If You Have Something to Say-

Say It!: The Complete Podcaster's Guide to Creating, Growing, and Monetizing Your Audience

By: M. D. Savant

2025

If you have ideas, thoughts, opinions, expertise - or you just like to talk - you can be a podcaster. Anyone who has anything to say about anything can find like-minded, or just curious, listeners. The size and scope of your audience is unlimited. And your audience is out there!

About the Author

M. D. Savant has twenty years of experience as a business and marketing consultant, specializing in social media platforms.

Welcome to the world of podcasting - a dynamic medium that has evolved from niche hobby to mainstream powerhouse. In this comprehensive guide, we'll explore how podcasting grew from its humble beginnings in the early 2000s to become a global phenomenon, and how you can harness its power to build your own successful show. Whether you're a complete beginner or looking to level up your existing podcast, this book will provide you with actionable strategies, technical know-how, and proven methods to create, grow, and monetize your podcast empire. From finding your unique voice to building a loyal community and generating revenue, we'll cover every aspect of podcast creation and management, helping you transform your passion into a thriving digital media business.

Table of Contents

Questions Answered in This Book

1. How can I start a podcast with minimal technical knowledge?
2. What are the key elements of building a strong podcast brand?
3. How can I adapt my podcast to audience feedback and industry trends?
4. What strategies can I use to develop and showcase my unique voice in podcasting?
5. What's the ideal balance between content strategy, technical skills, and marketing for podcast success?
6. What are the most effective ways to monetize a podcast?
7. How can I turn my podcast from a hobby into a viable business?
8. What are the best practices for content planning and time management in podcasting?
9. How can I improve my technical troubleshooting skills for smoother podcast production?
10. What strategies can I employ to build and engage a community around my podcast?
11. How do I find my audience?

Introduction

In the ever-evolving landscape of digital media, podcasting stands as a testament to the democratization of voice. What began in 2004 with a simple RSS feed modification has blossomed into a global phenomenon that gives anyone with a story, perspective, or passion the power to reach millions. As someone who has witnessed this transformation firsthand through my two decades in marketing and digital strategy, I've seen podcasting evolve from a niche hobby to a powerful medium that shapes conversations, builds communities, and launches careers.

When I first encountered podcasting, while advising a client on their digital strategy, I was admittedly skeptical. The idea of internet radio shows seemed like a passing trend. However, as I helped that client launch their show with just a USB microphone and free editing software, I witnessed something remarkable - the ability to build genuine connections with audiences worldwide without traditional media gatekeepers. That experience fundamentally changed my perspective on digital communication and shaped my approach to marketing strategy for years to come.

This book emerges from twenty years of observing, participating in, and guiding others through the podcasting landscape. It's designed to be your comprehensive companion in navigating every aspect of podcast creation, from technical setup to content strategy, from audience building to monetization. Whether you're a business professional looking to extend your reach, an enthusiast wanting to share your passion, or someone with a unique perspective seeking their voice, this guide will help you transform your podcast from concept to reality.

What sets podcasting apart from other media is its intimate nature - the direct connection between host and listener. This intimacy creates unprecedented opportunities for authentic engagement, but it also demands a thoughtful approach to content creation and audience building. Throughout these pages, we'll explore not just the how of podcasting, but the why - the strategic thinking that turns good shows into great ones, and great shows into sustainable successes.

In my years of consulting, I've seen countless podcasters struggle with common challenges: technical overwhelm, content consistency, audience growth, and monetization. This book addresses these challenges head-on, providing practical solutions drawn from real-world experience. You'll find actionable strategies, technical guidance, and proven frameworks that have helped numerous podcasters find their footing and build their audience.

Podcasting isn't just about broadcasting; it's about creating value for your listeners while building something meaningful for yourself. Whether your goal is to share your expertise, build a business, or simply connect with others who share your interests, the principles and strategies in this book will help you create a podcast that resonates with your intended audience and achieves your goals.

As we embark on this journey together, remember that every successful podcaster started exactly where you are now - with an idea and the desire to share it. The technical skills can be learned, the audience can be built, and the impact can be achieved. What matters most is your unique voice and perspective, combined with the right strategies and tools to bring it to the world.

Let's begin this adventure into podcasting - a medium that continues to evolve, surprise, and create opportunities for those ready to seize them. Your voice matters, and your audience is waiting to hear what you have to say. All you need is the right guidance to help you say it effectively.

1. The Podcast Revolution: From Past to Present and Your Place in It

In 2004, when the first RSS feed specifically designed for audio content emerged, few could have predicted how dramatically podcasting would transform the media landscape. What began as a niche technology experiment has evolved into a global phenomenon that gives voice to millions of creators and reaches billions of listeners across every conceivable topic and interest. This evolution represents one of the most significant shifts in media consumption and content creation of the 21st century. The technology that made podcasting possible emerged from a perfect storm of innovations - portable MP3 players, broadband internet, and RSS feed technology. But it was the human element - our fundamental desire to share stories and connect with others - that transformed podcasting from a tech curiosity into a cultural phenomenon.

When I first launched my marketing consultancy, I remember sitting in my office, surrounded by traditional media plans and print advertising mockups. A client approached me about a 'new type of radio show on the internet' they wanted to create. Initially skeptical, I spent weeks researching this emerging medium called podcasting. I discovered a small but passionate community of creators using basic equipment to reach audiences worldwide. Against conventional wisdom at the time, I helped my client launch their show using just a USB microphone and free editing software. Within six months, they had built a dedicated audience of industry professionals that transformed their business. That experience opened my eyes to podcasting's potential to democratize media and create meaningful connections. Now, two decades later, as I guide businesses through their digital strategies, I've seen countless similar stories of individuals and organizations using podcasting to find their voice and their audience. This personal journey from skeptic to advocate mirrors the broader evolution of podcasting itself - from experimental technology to essential communication channel.

Today's podcast landscape is remarkably different from those early days, yet the core appeal remains the same: the ability for anyone with a message to reach a global audience. The barriers to entry have dropped significantly, while the potential for impact and monetization has grown exponentially. Whether you're passionate about true crime, business strategy, cooking, or obscure historical events, there's likely an audience eager to hear your perspective.

In this chapter, we'll explore how podcasting has evolved from its humble beginnings to become a mainstream media force, and more importantly, we'll examine what this means for you as an aspiring or current podcaster. We'll look at how the democratization of audio content has created unprecedented opportunities for creators, and how you can position yourself within this dynamic medium, regardless of your technical expertise or subject matter focus.

The podcast revolution isn't just about technology or media consumption - it's about giving voice to ideas, stories, and perspectives that might otherwise go unheard. As we dive deeper into the history and current state of podcasting, you'll discover that success in this medium isn't reserved for celebrities or media professionals. It's available to anyone with something meaningful to say and the commitment to learn how to say it effectively.

The Birth and Evolution of Podcasting: Technical Foundations

The technical foundations of podcasting represent a fascinating convergence of multiple technologies that existed separately before coming together to create something entirely new. At its core, podcasting emerged from the combination of portable audio players, RSS feed technology, and the growing availability of broadband internet access. While these individual components had existed for years, it was their integration that sparked a media revolution.

In my early consulting days, I witnessed firsthand how these technologies were transforming the way people consumed and created content. I remember working with a client who was struggling to understand how RSS feeds worked. We spent an afternoon breaking down the concept using a simple analogy: imagine RSS as a newspaper delivery service for the internet. Just as a newspaper carrier knows exactly which houses to deliver to and when, RSS feeds automatically deliver new podcast episodes to subscribers. This fundamental technology remains at the heart of podcast distribution today, though it's now largely hidden behind user-friendly interfaces.

The evolution of audio compression technology, particularly the MP3 format, played a crucial role in making podcasting viable. This technology allowed creators to produce high-quality audio files small enough to be easily shared over the internet. When I first started helping clients with podcast production, we had to carefully balance audio quality with file size - a challenge that seems almost quaint by today's standards. Yet this technical constraint helped shape early podcast production practices, many of which still influence how we approach podcast creation today.

Perhaps the most significant technical development in podcasting's evolution was the emergence of specialized podcast hosting platforms. These services solved the bandwidth and storage challenges that had previously limited independent creators. I remember advising clients who were trying to host audio files on their own websites, watching their hosting costs skyrocket as their audience grew. The development of dedicated podcast hosting services democratized the medium by making it financially feasible for independent creators to reach large audiences.

- Key Technical Milestones in Podcasting:
- RSS feed technology adaptation for audio content
- Development of podcast-specific hosting platforms
- Integration with mobile devices and streaming services
- Standardization of audio formats and delivery methods
- Evolution of recording and editing software

The technical infrastructure of podcasting continues to evolve, with new innovations in audio processing, distribution, and analytics constantly emerging. Yet the fundamental principle remains unchanged: creating an accessible platform for voices to reach their audiences. As someone who has watched this evolution unfold, I'm continually amazed by how these technical foundations have enabled such a diverse and vibrant media ecosystem.

One of the most remarkable aspects of podcasting's technical evolution has been its ability to maintain backward compatibility while embracing new innovations. The basic RSS feed structure that powered early podcasts still works today, even as the industry has added support for enhanced features like chapters, transcripts, and dynamic ad insertion. This technical stability has been crucial in allowing creators to focus on content rather than constantly adapting to new technical requirements.

The democratization of podcast production tools has been equally important. When I first started helping clients create podcasts, we needed relatively sophisticated equipment and technical knowledge. Today, someone can start a podcast using just their smartphone and free editing software. This accessibility hasn't compromised quality - rather, it has allowed more diverse voices to enter the medium, each bringing their unique perspective and creativity.

As we look to the future, emerging technologies like AI-powered editing tools, improved speech-to-text capabilities, and enhanced analytics are making podcast production and distribution even more sophisticated. However, the core technical foundation remains remarkably similar to its origins - a testament to the robustness of podcasting's fundamental architecture.

From Niche to Mainstream: The Growth of Podcast Consumption

The transformation of podcasting from a niche hobby to a mainstream media format is one of the most remarkable shifts I've witnessed in my marketing career. When I first started advising clients about podcasting in the early 2000s, I had to spend considerable time explaining what a podcast actually was. Today, podcasting has become so ubiquitous that it's rare to meet someone who hasn't listened to at least one show.

I remember working with an early client who was skeptical about the medium's potential reach. "Who's going to listen to my show?" she asked. "Everyone's busy with radio and TV." We launched her business advice podcast anyway, and within two years, she had built a dedicated audience that far exceeded her initial expectations. Her story mirrors the broader trajectory of podcast consumption - from a tech-savvy niche audience to widespread mainstream adoption.

The growth of podcast consumption has been driven by several key factors. The rise of smartphones made podcasts easily accessible to listeners anywhere, anytime. The improvement in mobile internet connectivity removed the need to manually download episodes. And perhaps most importantly, the diversity of content has expanded to encompass virtually every topic imaginable.

- Key Factors in Mainstream Adoption:
- Improved accessibility through smartphones and apps
- Integration with car audio systems
- Voice-activated smart speakers
- Simplified user interfaces
- Higher production quality standards

As a marketing consultant, I've observed how this shift to mainstream consumption has transformed the opportunities available to creators. In the early days, podcasting was often seen as a supplementary marketing channel. Today, it's frequently the centerpiece of many successful media strategies. The intimacy of the audio format, combined with the convenience of on-demand listening, has created a unique value proposition that resonates with modern audiences.

The evolution of podcast consumption patterns has been equally fascinating. What started as primarily a tech-focused medium has expanded into every conceivable genre. I've helped clients launch successful shows in niches ranging from gardening to financial planning, each finding their dedicated audience. This diversification has been crucial in driving mainstream adoption, as potential listeners are now much more likely to find content that aligns with their interests.

One of the most significant aspects of this growth has been the shift in listening habits. Early podcast consumers typically had to be quite tech-savvy, manually downloading episodes and transferring them to portable devices. Today's listeners benefit from seamless streaming platforms that make discovering and consuming content as easy as pressing play. This reduction in technical barriers has been crucial in expanding the audience beyond early adopters to include listeners of all ages and technical abilities.

The mainstreaming of podcast consumption has also led to changes in content creation and distribution strategies. When I first started consulting, most podcasters were happy to reach a few hundred listeners. Now, the potential audience size is virtually unlimited, though success still depends on creating valuable content that resonates with your target audience. This shift has created new opportunities for creators while also raising the bar for production quality and content strategy.

As someone who has witnessed this evolution firsthand, I find it particularly rewarding to see how the growth in podcast consumption has validated the medium's potential. What was once dismissed as a passing fad has become an integral part of many people's daily media diet. The key lesson here for aspiring podcasters is that while the audience has grown tremendously, success still depends on creating content that adds value to listeners' lives.

The mainstream adoption of podcasting hasn't just changed how we consume content - it's transformed how we think about audio media entirely. The traditional barriers between professional and amateur content creators have blurred, creating unprecedented opportunities for new voices to reach significant audiences. This democratization of media creation and consumption continues to drive innovation in both content and delivery methods.

The Democratization of Audio Content Creation

The democratization of audio content creation represents one of the most significant shifts in media history. When I first entered the marketing and consulting field, audio production was largely confined to professional studios with expensive equipment and technical expertise. Today, that landscape has fundamentally changed, opening up unprecedented opportunities for creators of all backgrounds.

I recall working with a retired teacher who wanted to share her passion for local history. In the past, her stories might have remained confined to her classroom or local historical society meetings. Instead, with just a basic USB microphone and free editing software, she was able to create a compelling podcast that now reaches history enthusiasts across the globe. Her success story exemplifies how the barriers to entry in audio content creation have dramatically lowered.

The democratization of audio content creation has been driven by three key developments: the availability of affordable recording equipment, the emergence of user-friendly production software, and the proliferation of free distribution platforms. This combination has effectively removed the traditional gatekeepers who once controlled access to audio media production and distribution.

- Essential Elements of Democratized Audio Creation:
- Accessible recording equipment at various price points
- Free or low-cost editing software options
- Multiple distribution platform choices
- Educational resources and community support
- Simple monetization pathways

The impact of this democratization extends far beyond just making it easier to create content. It has fundamentally changed who gets to have a voice in the media landscape.

When I started my consulting practice, I primarily worked with established businesses and organizations. Now, I regularly advise individuals from all walks of life who are using podcasting to share their expertise, tell their stories, or build communities around shared interests.

One of the most powerful aspects of this democratization has been the way it has enabled niche content creation. In the traditional broadcast model, content needed to appeal to broad audiences to justify production costs. Today, creators can successfully serve smaller, highly engaged audiences with specific interests. I've seen this firsthand with clients who have built successful shows around topics that would never have found a home in traditional media.

The democratization of audio content has also led to more diverse and representative voices in the media landscape. When the barriers to entry are lowered, we hear from people and perspectives that might otherwise have gone unheard. This diversity enriches the podcast ecosystem and creates more opportunities for meaningful connections between creators and listeners.

The tools and platforms that enable this democratization continue to evolve and improve. What started with basic recording apps and simple hosting solutions has grown into a sophisticated ecosystem of production tools, analytics platforms, and monetization options. Yet importantly, the core principle remains the same: anyone with a story to tell or knowledge to share can find their audience through podcasting.

This democratization has also fostered a supportive community of creators who share knowledge and resources. I've watched as podcast creators, regardless of their experience level or audience size, help each other solve technical challenges, share promotion strategies, and offer encouragement. This collaborative spirit has been crucial in making podcasting more accessible to newcomers.

The future of audio content creation looks even more promising as new technologies continue to lower barriers and expand possibilities. From AI-powered editing tools to improved analytics and audience engagement features, the tools available to independent creators are becoming increasingly sophisticated. However, the fundamental democratizing principle remains unchanged - the power to create and distribute audio content rests in the hands of anyone willing to learn and engage with the medium.

Understanding Today's Podcast Ecosystem

Today's podcast ecosystem is a complex and dynamic landscape that bears little resemblance to the medium's early days. As someone who has navigated these changes alongside numerous clients, I've watched the transformation from a relatively simple environment of RSS feeds and direct downloads to a sophisticated network of creators, platforms, advertisers, and listeners.

When I first started consulting in the podcast space, the ecosystem was straightforward - creators would host their audio files, generate an RSS feed, and listeners would download episodes through iTunes or similar applications. Now, we operate in a multi-layered environment where content creation, distribution, monetization, and consumption are interconnected in increasingly complex ways.

One of my early clients struggled to understand this evolving ecosystem. She was an experienced radio broadcaster who assumed podcasting would follow the same rules and structures as traditional radio. I remember spending an afternoon mapping out the podcast ecosystem on her office whiteboard, showing how different elements - from hosting platforms to analytics tools to monetization channels - worked together. This visual representation helped her understand that podcasting wasn't just radio on the internet, but rather a distinct medium with its own rules and opportunities.

- Key Components of Today's Podcast Ecosystem:
- Content Creation Tools and Platforms
- Hosting and Distribution Networks
- Discovery and Listening Platforms
- Analytics and Measurement Systems
- Monetization and Marketing Channels

The modern podcast ecosystem is built on a foundation of specialized services and platforms that handle different aspects of the podcasting process. Hosting platforms manage storage and delivery, analytics services track listener behavior, and monetization platforms connect creators with advertising opportunities. This specialization has made it easier for new podcasters to enter the medium while providing established creators with tools to grow their shows.

One of the most significant changes I've observed in the podcast ecosystem is the rise of platform-specific features and exclusive content. While the open RSS standard remains the backbone of podcast distribution, major platforms have introduced proprietary features and exclusive shows that create new opportunities - and challenges - for creators. This evolution has added complexity to the ecosystem while also expanding the possibilities for audience growth and monetization.

The relationship between creators and listeners has also evolved within this ecosystem. In the early days, interaction was largely one-directional, with limited feedback channels between podcasters and their audience. Today's ecosystem supports multiple touchpoints for engagement, from social media integration to community platforms to live events. This multi-channel approach has transformed podcasting from a purely audio medium to a broader content and community experience.

As a consultant, I've found that understanding the podcast ecosystem is crucial for success in the medium. Each element - from hosting to analytics to monetization - plays a vital role in a show's growth and sustainability. The ecosystem's complexity can seem daunting at first, but it also provides creators with more tools and opportunities than ever before.

The current podcast ecosystem also includes a robust support structure of service providers, from editing and production services to marketing and promotion specialists. This professional infrastructure has made it possible for creators to focus on content while outsourcing technical and operational aspects of their shows. I've watched numerous clients benefit from this evolving support system, allowing them to scale their podcasts without becoming overwhelmed by technical or operational challenges.

Looking ahead, the podcast ecosystem continues to evolve with new technologies and business models emerging regularly. From improved discovery algorithms to innovative monetization methods, the opportunities for creators continue to expand. However, the fundamental principle remains unchanged - success in podcasting comes from understanding how to effectively navigate and leverage the various components of the ecosystem while staying focused on creating valuable content for your audience.

Identifying Your Unique Position in the Podcast Space

Finding your unique position in the podcast space begins with understanding a fundamental truth I've observed over two decades of consulting: authenticity resonates more powerfully than imitation. Early in my consulting career, I worked with a client who was determined to create a business podcast that mimicked the style of popular shows in the space. Despite her expertise in sustainable business practices, she felt compelled to adopt a more conventional approach. The result was a show that felt forced and failed to connect with listeners. Everything changed when we refocused on her unique perspective and passionate advocacy for environmental entrepreneurship. By embracing her distinctive voice and expertise, she created a show that stood out in the crowded business podcast landscape.

Your unique position in the podcast space emerges from the intersection of your expertise, passion, and perspective. Think of it as your podcast's DNA - the distinctive combination of elements that makes your show uniquely valuable to your target audience. This isn't just about choosing a niche topic; it's about bringing your authentic voice and perspective to that topic in a way that adds value for your listeners.

- Elements of a Strong Podcast Position:
- Authentic voice and perspective
- Clear value proposition for listeners
- Distinctive approach to your chosen topic
- Consistent brand identity
- Defined target audience focus

When helping clients identify their podcast positioning, I often use an exercise I call the 'Three Circles.' Draw three overlapping circles labeled 'Expertise,' 'Passion,' and 'Market Need.' Your sweet spot - your unique position - lies where these circles intersect. This approach has helped countless creators move beyond generic show concepts to develop truly distinctive podcasts that serve specific audience needs.

The podcast space has room for multiple voices covering similar topics, but success comes from finding your unique angle. I remember working with two clients who both wanted to create shows about personal finance. Instead of competing directly with established finance podcasts, we helped each identify their unique perspective. One focused on financial strategies for creative entrepreneurs, drawing from her background as both an accountant and former artist. The other developed a show about sustainable investing, combining his financial expertise with his passion for environmental issues. Both found success by positioning themselves distinctively within the broader personal finance category.

Your position in the podcast space should also reflect your authentic personality and communication style. Trying to adopt a persona that doesn't align with your natural way of engaging with others rarely works long-term. I've seen too many podcasters burn out trying to maintain an artificial personality or forced style. The most sustainable and successful shows are those where the host's authentic voice shines through.

Consider what specific value you can offer that isn't currently being served in your chosen area. This doesn't mean you need to invent a completely new category of podcast. Rather, think about how your unique combination of experiences, knowledge, and perspective can add value to existing conversations. What questions can you answer? What problems can you solve? What perspectives can you share that might be missing from current discussions?

The process of finding your unique position isn't just about differentiation - it's about creating genuine value for your listeners. I often advise clients to start by identifying the specific problems or needs their target audience faces. Then, consider how your particular background, expertise, or perspective enables you to address those needs in a way others might not.

Remember that your unique position can evolve as you grow and learn from your audience. Some of the most successful podcasters I've worked with started with one positioning and gradually refined it based on listener feedback and their own developing interests. The key is to start from a place of authenticity and remain open to evolution while maintaining your core value proposition.

Your position in the podcast space should also consider the practical aspects of sustaining and growing your show. Can you consistently create content from this position? Does it align with your long-term goals? Does it provide opportunities for monetization if that's important to you? These practical considerations help ensure your unique position is not just distinctive but sustainable.

The podcast medium offers unprecedented opportunities for niche content and specialized perspectives. Unlike traditional broadcast media, which often requires broad appeal, podcasting allows you to serve specific audiences with targeted content. This makes it possible to build a successful show around highly focused topics or unique approaches that might not work in other media formats. The key is identifying where your authentic voice and expertise intersect with an audience's needs and interests.

The Future of Podcasting and Emerging Opportunities

As we look toward the future of podcasting, we're entering an era of unprecedented opportunity and innovation. When I first started advising clients about podcast strategy, the technology was relatively simple - a microphone, basic editing software, and an RSS feed were all you needed. Today, we're seeing the emergence of technologies and trends that are reshaping what's possible in the medium.

I recently worked with a client who was concerned about investing in podcast equipment, worried that the medium might be reaching its peak. I shared with her what I've observed over two decades in digital marketing: podcasting isn't just surviving - it's continuously evolving and creating new opportunities for creators. From improved discovery algorithms to AI-powered production tools, the technological foundations of podcasting are becoming more sophisticated while paradoxically becoming easier to use.

The future of podcasting is being shaped by several key technological and cultural shifts. Voice-activated devices and smart speakers are making podcast consumption more seamless than ever. The integration of podcasting into connected cars is expanding listening opportunities. And improvements in recommendation engines are making it easier for listeners to discover content that matches their interests.

- Emerging Opportunities in Podcasting:
- Interactive and dynamic content delivery
- Enhanced analytics and listener insights
- Improved discovery mechanisms
- Integration with emerging technologies
- New monetization models

One of the most exciting developments I'm seeing is the emergence of dynamic content delivery. This technology allows podcasters to create more personalized listening experiences, with content that adapts based on listener preferences or behavior. While working with a weather-focused podcast client, we implemented dynamic content insertion that customized certain segments based on the listener's location - a small taste of what's possible with this technology.

The rise of social audio platforms and live streaming capabilities is also creating new opportunities for podcast creators to engage with their audiences in real-time. This convergence of live and recorded content is opening up new possibilities for community building and audience engagement. I've helped several clients integrate live elements into their podcast strategy, creating powerful feedback loops that inform and improve their recorded content.

Artificial intelligence and machine learning are beginning to transform various aspects of podcast production and distribution. From automated transcription and translation services to AI-powered editing tools, these technologies are making it easier for creators to focus on content while automating technical tasks. However, I always remind my clients that while AI can enhance production efficiency, it can't replace the human elements that make podcasting powerful - authentic voices, genuine connections, and compelling storytelling.

The future of podcast monetization is also evolving beyond traditional advertising models. We're seeing the emergence of hybrid revenue streams that combine advertising, premium content, merchandise, and community-based support systems. This diversification of revenue opportunities is making it possible for more creators to build sustainable podcast businesses.

As someone who has watched the podcast industry evolve from its earliest days, I'm particularly excited about the democratizing effect of these emerging technologies and platforms. New tools are making it easier than ever for voices that might have gone unheard to find their audience. Recently, I worked with a client who used automated translation tools to make their podcast accessible to Spanish-speaking listeners, effectively doubling their potential audience overnight.

The future of podcasting isn't just about technology - it's about the continuing evolution of how we create and consume audio content. The lines between different forms of audio media are blurring, creating new hybrid formats and opportunities for innovation. Whether it's the integration of visual elements, the expansion of interactive features, or the development of new distribution channels, the podcast medium continues to expand its capabilities while maintaining its core strength: the intimate connection between creator and listener.

For aspiring and current podcasters, these emerging opportunities represent both challenges and possibilities. The key to success will be maintaining authenticity and value while strategically adopting new technologies and approaches that enhance the listener experience. As I tell my clients, the future of podcasting belongs to those who can balance innovation with the fundamental principles of good content creation.

The podcast landscape of tomorrow will likely look very different from today, just as today's environment is dramatically different from when I first entered the field. Yet the core appeal of the medium - the ability to create meaningful connections through audio content - remains unchanged. The emerging opportunities in podcasting are tools that enhance this fundamental strength, not replacements for it.As we conclude this exploration of podcasting's evolution and current landscape, it's clear that we're in the midst of a transformative period in media history. From its humble beginnings as an experimental technology in 2004, podcasting has grown into a global phenomenon that continues to reshape how we create, consume, and share content. Through my journey from skeptical consultant to passionate advocate, I've witnessed firsthand how this medium has broken down traditional barriers to audio content creation and distribution.

The technical foundations we explored - from RSS feeds to specialized hosting platforms - have evolved to create an increasingly accessible medium. What started as a complex technical endeavor requiring significant expertise has become a medium that welcomes creators of all technical backgrounds. This democratization of audio content creation has opened doors for diverse voices and perspectives that might never have found a platform in traditional media.

As we've discussed throughout this chapter, the current podcast ecosystem offers unprecedented opportunities for creators to find and serve their audiences. The transformation from niche technology to mainstream medium hasn't just changed how we consume content - it's revolutionized who gets to create it. Whether you're an entrepreneur sharing business insights, a teacher expanding your classroom's reach, or simply someone with a story to tell, there's space for your voice in the podcasting landscape.

Looking ahead, the future of podcasting promises even more innovations and opportunities. From improved discovery mechanisms to new monetization models, the medium continues to evolve while maintaining its core strength: the ability to create meaningful connections through audio content. The key lesson from this chapter isn't just about understanding the history and current state of podcasting - it's about recognizing that you're entering the medium at a time of unprecedented opportunity.

As you move forward in your podcasting journey, remember that success in this medium isn't about having the most expensive equipment or the largest initial audience. It's about finding your authentic voice, understanding your unique position in the podcast space, and consistently delivering value to your listeners. The technical and creative tools available today make it possible for anyone with passion and dedication to create a successful podcast.

The podcast revolution we've explored in this chapter isn't just about technology or media consumption - it's about the democratization of voice. As we move into the next chapter, where we'll dive into the practical aspects of podcast creation, keep in mind that you're not just learning how to use a set of tools - you're preparing to add your unique voice to a global conversation.

2. Your Podcast Launch Formula: Equipment, Setup, and Technical Foundations

The difference between a professional-sounding podcast and an amateur production often comes down to just a few key technical decisions made at the outset. While the equipment landscape can seem overwhelming, creating a high-quality podcast setup doesn't require a recording studio's worth of gear - it just requires the right knowledge to make smart choices. What I've learned over two decades of consulting is that success in podcasting isn't about having the most expensive setup - it's about making smart choices with whatever resources you have available. The technical foundations of your podcast will either set you up for long-term success or create ongoing challenges that can derail your progress.

When podcasting first emerged, creators were working with basic USB microphones and free recording software, yet they managed to build engaged audiences through compelling content and consistent delivery. Today's podcasters have access to an incredible array of equipment and software options, but the fundamental principles of quality audio production remain unchanged.

Early in my consulting career, I was working with a client who had invested thousands in top-of-the-line podcast equipment before even recording their first episode. They had the most expensive microphone, a professional mixing board, and acoustic panels covering every wall - yet their test recordings sounded terrible. When I visited their setup, I discovered they were recording in a room with hardwood floors and bare walls behind their microphone, creating harsh echoes that no amount of expensive gear could fix. We solved the problem with a $30 carpet remnant and strategically placed cushions from their living room couch. That experience taught me a valuable lesson I've shared with countless clients since: it's not about having the most expensive equipment, but rather understanding how to use what you have effectively. We ended up selling most of their high-end gear and creating a simpler, more effective setup that produced excellent audio quality at a fraction of the cost. This experience fundamentally shaped how I approach podcast technical setup with all my clients - focus on the fundamentals first, then upgrade strategically as needed.

In this chapter, we'll explore the essential technical elements needed to launch your podcast, from selecting the right equipment for your budget to optimizing your recording space. I'll share practical insights on choosing microphones, audio interfaces, and software that align with your goals and technical comfort level. Most importantly, you'll learn how to avoid common technical pitfalls that can impact your show's audio quality and production efficiency.

Whether you're starting with a basic setup or planning to invest in professional equipment, understanding these technical foundations will help you make informed decisions that support your podcast's growth. Let's begin by examining the core equipment choices that will form the backbone of your podcast production setup.

Essential Recording Equipment: Microphones, Interfaces, and Accessories
When I first started advising clients about podcast equipment in the early 2000s, the options were limited and often expensive. Today, the market offers an incredible range of recording gear at every price point. However, this abundance of choice can feel overwhelming for new podcasters. Let me simplify the essential equipment you'll need to get started with professional-quality audio.

Let's start with the most crucial piece of equipment - your microphone. There are two main categories of microphones you'll encounter: USB and XLR. USB microphones plug directly into your computer and are perfect for beginners. They're simple to use, require minimal additional equipment, and can produce excellent audio quality. The downside is they offer less flexibility for upgrading your setup later. XLR microphones, while requiring an audio interface to connect to your computer, provide superior audio quality and more control over your sound. They're the standard in professional audio production but come with a steeper learning curve and higher initial investment.

I remember working with a client who was adamant about starting with high-end XLR equipment, despite having no audio experience. After struggling with the technical complexity, they switched to a quality USB microphone and found immediate success. The lesson was clear - starting with simpler equipment that you can use effectively is better than having professional gear you can't fully utilize.

For those starting out, I recommend investing in a good quality USB condenser microphone. These microphones are sensitive enough to capture the nuances of your voice while being forgiving enough for home recording environments. Look for models that include a built-in pop filter and shock mount to reduce unwanted noise.

If you're ready for an XLR setup, you'll need an audio interface - the device that connects your microphone to your computer. Choose an interface with at least two inputs if you plan to record in-person interviews or multiple hosts. The interface should provide phantom power (usually labeled as +48V) for condenser microphones and offer good preamps for clean signal amplification.

Don't overlook the importance of accessories. A sturdy microphone stand keeps your mic in the optimal position and prevents handling noise. Pop filters reduce plosive sounds (those harsh 'p' and 'b' sounds), while shock mounts minimize vibrations from your desk or floor. A good pair of closed-back headphones is essential for monitoring your audio during recording and editing.

One often-overlooked but crucial accessory is proper cabling. I've seen countless recording sessions derailed by cheap cables that introduce noise or fail mid-recording. Invest in quality XLR cables if you're using an XLR microphone, and always have backups on hand.

When it comes to storing and transporting your equipment, consider investing in protective cases or bags. I learned this lesson the hard way when a client's expensive microphone was damaged during transport because it was poorly packed. Quality cases not only protect your investment but also help organize your gear for remote recording sessions.

Remember, your equipment needs will likely evolve as your podcast grows. Start with the basics that match your current skill level and budget, then upgrade strategically as you identify specific needs or limitations in your setup. The goal is to have reliable equipment that helps you focus on creating great content rather than fighting with technical issues.

In my experience, the most successful podcasters are those who master their basic equipment before moving to more advanced setups. They understand that great content recorded on modest gear will always outperform mediocre content captured with expensive equipment. Focus on learning to use your initial setup effectively, and you'll be well-positioned to make informed decisions about future upgrades.

Creating Your Home Recording Space: Acoustics and Setup

Your recording space can make or break your podcast's sound quality, regardless of how expensive your equipment might be. I learned this lesson early in my consulting career when a client's expensive microphone setup was being ruined by a noisy air conditioning unit and room echo. The solution wasn't more gear - it was understanding and optimizing their recording environment.

The first step in creating your recording space is choosing the right room. Look for a quiet area away from external noise sources like street traffic, appliances, and HVAC systems. Smaller rooms are often better than large ones, as they have less space for sound to bounce around. If possible, avoid rooms with parallel walls and lots of hard, reflective surfaces.

When I first started helping clients set up their recording spaces, I was amazed at how everyday household items could be used to improve acoustics. Soft furnishings like curtains, carpets, and cushions naturally absorb sound reflections. Bookshelves filled with books create irregular surfaces that help diffuse sound waves. Even hanging clothes in a closet can create an effective recording booth.

Here's a simple test I use with clients to evaluate room acoustics: clap your hands once sharply and listen to the sound decay. In an untreated room, you'll hear a distinct echo or 'ring.' The goal is to minimize this reflection while maintaining some natural warmth in your voice recording.

Basic acoustic treatment doesn't have to be expensive. Start by identifying the main reflection points - typically the walls directly beside and behind your microphone, and the ceiling above. These are the surfaces where sound waves bounce back to your microphone most directly. Here are some effective solutions I've used with clients:

- Hang heavy blankets or moving pads on walls
- Place foam panels at key reflection points
- Position your desk and microphone away from walls
- Use a reflection filter behind your microphone
- Place rugs or carpet on hard floors

Your microphone positioning is crucial in your recording space. I recommend setting up your microphone in the center of the room, away from walls and corners where sound tends to build up. Position yourself so you're speaking past the microphone rather than directly into it - this helps reduce plosive sounds and gives your voice a more natural quality.

One often overlooked aspect of recording space setup is desk noise. Your microphone can pick up vibrations from typing, mouse clicks, or even resting your arms on the desk. I always recommend using a proper microphone stand rather than a desk-mounted option, and placing a thick mouse pad or foam sheet under your work area to dampen vibrations.

Temperature control is another important consideration. I once worked with a client whose recordings were consistently interrupted by their noisy air conditioning unit. We developed a routine of recording during the cooler morning hours and using a small, quiet fan for comfort during longer sessions. If you must run air conditioning while recording, try to position your microphone as far as possible from vents and consider using a noise gate in your recording software.

Organization is key to a functional recording space. Create a dedicated area for your equipment that allows easy access while keeping cables tidy and out of the way. I recommend using velcro cable ties and running cables along desk edges or walls to prevent tripping hazards and reduce handling noise.

Remember that your recording space doesn't need to be perfect - it just needs to be consistent. Some of the most successful podcasts started in makeshift spaces with basic acoustic treatment. The key is understanding how your space affects your sound and making strategic improvements over time.

Keep in mind that your recording environment might need to evolve as your podcast grows. Start with the basics - controlling room reflections and external noise - and make incremental improvements as you identify specific issues in your recordings. The goal is to create a comfortable, reliable space where you can focus on creating great content without fighting against poor acoustics or environmental distractions.

Digital Audio Workstations (DAW) and Recording Software
Choosing the right Digital Audio Workstation (DAW) and recording software is crucial for creating professional-quality podcast episodes. When I first started advising clients about podcast production, we were limited to basic audio editors with minimal features. Today's podcasters have access to sophisticated DAWs that offer everything from basic recording to advanced audio processing capabilities.

Your DAW will be the central hub of your podcast production workflow. It's where you'll record, edit, mix, and export your episodes. While the choices might seem overwhelming, I've found that the best DAW for podcasting is often the one you can learn to use effectively rather than the one with the most features.

For beginners, I recommend starting with user-friendly software that focuses on podcast-specific features. These programs typically offer intuitive interfaces, basic editing tools, and essential audio processing capabilities without overwhelming you with complex features you may never use. I remember working with a client who initially struggled with a professional-grade DAW, spending more time fighting the software than creating content.

After switching to a simpler, podcast-focused platform, their production time was cut in half, and their audio quality actually improved.

When evaluating recording software, consider these essential features:

- Multi-track recording capabilities for interviews and multiple hosts
- Basic editing tools for cutting, copying, and moving audio
- Built-in audio processing tools like EQ and compression
- Noise reduction capabilities
- The ability to export in podcast-friendly formats
- Automated backup features to prevent lost work

One of the most valuable lessons I've learned is the importance of choosing software that matches your technical comfort level. I once had a client who insisted on using a complex professional DAW because that's what their favorite podcaster used. After weeks of frustration and delayed episodes, they switched to a simpler platform that met their needs without the steep learning curve.

Your recording software should also integrate well with your existing workflow. Consider how you'll record remote guests, handle file backups, and export your final episodes. Some DAWs offer direct integration with podcast hosting platforms, making the publishing process more streamlined.

For remote recording, many podcasters now use specialized web-based platforms that record each participant locally while maintaining high audio quality. These services often integrate with traditional DAWs, allowing you to easily import the separate audio tracks for editing and mixing.

Storage and organization features are crucial for long-term podcast production. Look for software that offers clear file management systems and the ability to create templates for consistent episode formatting. I advise my clients to establish a standardized naming convention for their project files and to maintain organized folders for episodes, assets, and backup files.

When it comes to audio processing, modern DAWs offer powerful tools for enhancing your podcast's sound quality. However, it's important not to get carried away with processing. I've seen many podcasters apply too many effects in an attempt to sound 'professional,' only to end up with unnatural, over-processed audio. Remember that the goal is to achieve clear, consistent audio that serves your content, not to showcase every audio effect in your software.

Consider your future needs when choosing a DAW. While you might start with basic recording and editing, you may eventually want to incorporate music, sound effects, or more complex production elements. Choosing software that can grow with your podcast can save you the hassle of switching platforms later.

Most importantly, take time to learn your chosen software thoroughly. Understanding your DAW's capabilities and limitations will help you work more efficiently and solve technical problems when they arise. I always recommend that my clients spend at least a few hours practicing with sample recordings before attempting their first real episode. This investment in learning pays dividends in smoother production workflows and better-quality output.

Remember that no software is perfect, and there's no single 'best' DAW for podcasting. The right choice depends on your specific needs, technical skills, and production goals. Focus on finding software that supports your creative process rather than complicating it with unnecessary features.

Audio Processing Fundamentals: EQ, Compression, and Noise Reduction

Understanding audio processing fundamentals is crucial for achieving professional-quality podcast sound. When I first started consulting, many of my clients were intimidated by terms like EQ, compression, and noise reduction. However, these tools are simply ways to shape and enhance your recorded audio - think of them as the seasonings that help make your podcast more palatable for listeners.

Let's start with equalization (EQ), which allows you to adjust different frequency ranges in your audio. Think of EQ like a mixing board where you can turn up or down specific parts of the sound spectrum. In podcasting, we primarily use EQ to enhance voice clarity and remove unwanted frequencies. I remember working with a client whose voice recordings sounded muddy and unclear. By applying a slight boost around 2-3 kHz (where human speech intelligibility lives) and cutting some low frequencies around 100-200 Hz, we dramatically improved the clarity of their voice while maintaining its natural character.

Compression is another essential tool that helps control the dynamic range of your audio - the difference between the loudest and quietest parts. A good compressor acts like an automatic volume control, turning down the loud peaks and bringing up quieter sections. This creates more consistent audio levels that are easier for listeners to follow. Early in my career, I worked with a podcast host who had a very dynamic speaking style, going from whispers to excited exclamations. We used compression to tame these variations while preserving the natural enthusiasm in their delivery.

One of the most common challenges in podcast audio is dealing with unwanted background noise. Noise reduction tools help remove consistent background sounds like computer fans, air conditioning, or room tone. However, it's important to use these tools carefully. I once helped a client who had applied aggressive noise reduction to fix a noisy recording, only to end up with audio that sounded artificial and processed. We found better results by re-recording in a quieter environment and using minimal noise reduction.

Here are some key principles for effective audio processing:

- Start with subtle adjustments and increase gradually as needed

- Always trust your ears over visual meters or preset settings
- Process during recording when possible to minimize post-production work
- Keep a reference track of unprocessed audio for comparison
- Save your processing chains as templates for consistency across episodes

The goal of audio processing isn't to create perfectly clean sound - it's to enhance the natural qualities of your voice while minimizing distractions for your listeners. I advise my clients to think of audio processing as enhancement rather than correction. The best processing is often subtle enough that listeners don't notice it's there, they just enjoy clear, professional-sounding audio.

When setting up your processing chain, start with noise reduction (if needed), followed by EQ, and finally compression. This order typically produces the most natural results. For EQ, begin by cutting problematic frequencies rather than boosting - this helps avoid adding unwanted noise or distortion to your signal. With compression, start with gentle settings (2:1 or 3:1 ratio) and adjust the threshold until you're catching just the loudest peaks.

Remember that different voices and recording environments may require different processing approaches. What works perfectly for one podcast might sound terrible on another. Take time to experiment with different settings and combinations until you find what works best for your specific situation. Keep notes about successful settings so you can maintain consistency across episodes.

One common mistake I see is podcasters trying to fix poor recordings with processing. While these tools can help improve your audio, they can't fix fundamental problems like bad microphone technique or poor room acoustics. Always focus on getting the best possible recording first, then use processing to enhance rather than rescue your audio.

The key to mastering audio processing is practice and patience. Start with basic adjustments and gradually explore more advanced techniques as you become comfortable with the fundamentals. Listen to your processed audio on different devices - headphones, car speakers, phone speakers - to ensure your processing choices translate well across various listening environments.

Most importantly, don't get caught up in endless tweaking. While it's important to have good sound quality, remember that your content is what ultimately keeps listeners engaged. Find a processing setup that works well for your voice and stick with it, allowing you to focus more energy on creating compelling content for your audience.

Remote Recording Solutions and Multi-Guest Setup
Recording remote guests and managing multi-person setups has become increasingly important in modern podcasting. When I first started consulting, remote recording meant dealing with choppy Skype calls and inconsistent audio quality. Today, we have sophisticated tools and platforms specifically designed for podcast recording across

distances, making it possible to produce professional-quality content with participants from anywhere in the world.

One of my earliest experiences with remote recording involved helping a client coordinate a podcast episode with guests in three different time zones. We initially tried using basic video conferencing software, but the audio quality was poor and unusable. This led us to explore dedicated podcast recording platforms that capture each participant's audio locally - a game-changing approach that dramatically improved the final product.

When setting up for remote recording, consider these essential elements:

- A stable, high-speed internet connection
- A quiet recording environment for all participants
- Quality headphones to prevent audio feedback
- A backup recording method
- Clear communication protocols for participants

The technology for remote recording has evolved significantly since podcasting's early days. In those days, podcasters were limited to recording phone calls or internet voice chat. Today's dedicated podcast recording platforms offer features like separate track recording, backup systems, and even studio-quality processing tools.

I always advise my clients to conduct a test recording session before any important remote interview. This allows you to identify and address technical issues, ensure all participants are comfortable with the platform, and establish clear communication protocols. During one consulting session, I worked with a podcast host who learned this lesson the hard way after losing an hour-long interview with an important guest due to unchecked technical issues.

For multi-guest setups, whether remote or in-person, organization is crucial. Create a pre-recording checklist that includes:

- Testing each participant's audio levels
- Confirming backup recording systems are running
- Establishing clear signals for technical difficulties
- Setting guidelines for turn-taking and interruptions
- Arranging a backup communication channel

When recording multiple guests in-person, microphone selection and placement become critical. I recommend using individual microphones for each participant rather than trying to share or use omnidirectional mics. This gives you more control during editing and helps maintain consistent audio quality.

Remote recording platforms have become increasingly sophisticated, offering features like:

- Individual track recording for each participant
- Built-in backup systems

- Real-time monitoring tools
- Integration with popular DAWs
- Progressive upload to prevent data loss

One of the most valuable lessons I've learned about remote recording is the importance of preparation. I now provide my clients with a guest preparation guide that includes technical requirements, environment setup tips, and communication protocols. This simple step has dramatically reduced technical issues and improved recording quality.

For multi-guest episodes, consider implementing a 'virtual green room' practice where participants join the session 15-20 minutes early for technical checks and brief orientation. This helps ensure everyone is comfortable with the technology and understands the recording process before going live.

Remember that different recording situations may require different approaches. While recording remotely, it's essential to have a backup recording method - I often recommend that each participant record their audio locally as a safeguard against internet issues or platform failures. For in-person multi-guest sessions, having spare microphones and cables readily available can save an entire recording session.

The key to successful remote and multi-guest recording is establishing clear protocols and backup systems. Train your guests on proper microphone technique, how to check their internet connection, and what to do if technical issues arise. Having these systems in place allows you to focus on creating engaging content rather than troubleshooting technical problems.

Most importantly, remember that technical perfection shouldn't come at the expense of natural conversation. While it's important to maintain good audio quality, don't let technical considerations overshadow the human element of your podcast. Some of the most engaging episodes I've helped produce had minor technical imperfections but captured authentic, compelling conversations.

As remote recording technology continues to evolve, stay informed about new tools and platforms that could enhance your podcast production. However, don't feel pressured to adopt every new technology - focus on finding reliable solutions that work for your specific needs and technical comfort level.

Backup Systems and Technical Troubleshooting

In my twenty years of consulting, I've learned that the difference between a successful podcast and one that fails often comes down to having robust backup systems and troubleshooting protocols in place. Nothing derails a podcast's momentum quite like lost episodes or technical failures that could have been prevented with proper planning.

I vividly remember working with a client who lost three weeks of carefully crafted episodes when their hard drive failed. They had no backup system in place, and the recovery process was both expensive and unsuccessful. This experience taught me the vital importance of implementing comprehensive backup strategies from day one.

Let's start with the fundamental rule of podcast backup: the 3-2-1 principle. Keep at least three copies of your podcast files, store them on two different types of media, and keep one copy off-site. This might sound excessive, but I've seen this system save countless podcasters from disaster. Here's how to implement it effectively:

- Maintain a primary working copy on your main computer
- Keep a local backup on an external hard drive
- Store another copy in cloud storage
- Archive final episodes on a separate dedicated drive
- Consider keeping raw recordings separate from edited files

When it comes to technical troubleshooting, prevention is always better than cure. Develop a pre-recording checklist that includes:

- Testing all equipment connections
- Checking audio levels and recording software settings
- Verifying backup systems are running
- Ensuring sufficient storage space is available
- Confirming all necessary software updates are complete

One of the most valuable lessons I've learned about technical troubleshooting is the importance of methodical problem-solving. When issues arise, resist the urge to make multiple changes at once. Address one potential problem at a time, testing after each adjustment. This systematic approach helps identify the root cause more quickly and prevents creating new issues while trying to solve existing ones.

Create a troubleshooting log to track common technical issues and their solutions. This becomes an invaluable resource when problems recur and helps identify patterns that might indicate equipment needing replacement or maintenance. I advise my clients to note:

- The specific nature of the problem
- Any error messages received
- Steps taken to resolve the issue
- The final solution that worked
- Any preventive measures implemented

For live recording sessions, always have backup equipment ready. This includes:

- A spare microphone
- Extra XLR cables
- Backup headphones
- Alternative recording device

- Portable power bank

One often overlooked aspect of technical preparation is software redundancy. I recommend having at least two ways to record your podcast. If your primary DAW fails, you should be able to quickly switch to an alternative recording method without losing the session. This might mean having a simple audio recorder running alongside your main recording software.

Regular maintenance is crucial for preventing technical issues. Schedule monthly checks of your equipment and backup systems. Clean your equipment, test all connections, and verify that your backup systems are functioning correctly. During one consulting session, we discovered a client's automatic cloud backup had stopped working three months earlier - fortunately before any data was lost.

When technical issues do arise, stay calm and methodical. I teach my clients the STOP method:

- Stop what you're doing
- Think about what changed recently
- Observe all indicators and settings
- Plan your troubleshooting steps before acting

Keep detailed documentation of your technical setup, including:

- Equipment serial numbers and purchase dates
- Software versions and settings
- Connection diagrams
- Backup system configurations
- Emergency contact information for technical support

Remember that even the most well-maintained systems can fail. The goal isn't to prevent every possible technical issue - that's impossible. Instead, focus on creating robust systems that can handle failures without derailing your podcast production schedule. Having proper backup systems and troubleshooting protocols in place gives you the confidence to focus on creating great content rather than worrying about technical disasters.

Most importantly, regularly test your backup and recovery procedures. Don't wait until you need them to discover they're not working as expected. Schedule quarterly practice runs of your backup recovery process to ensure you can restore your files if needed. This practice has saved numerous clients from potentially catastrophic data loss situations. When podcasting first emerged, most podcasters were working with basic USB microphones and free recording software, yet they managed to build engaged audiences through compelling content and consistent delivery. Today, while we have access to sophisticated equipment and advanced software, the fundamental principles of quality audio production remain unchanged. The technical foundations you establish for your podcast will either propel you toward success or create ongoing challenges that hinder your progress.

Throughout this chapter, we've explored the essential elements needed to create a professional-sounding podcast, from selecting appropriate equipment to optimizing your recording space. We've learned that success isn't about having the most expensive setup - it's about making informed choices with whatever resources you have available.

Remember the story of my client who invested thousands in top-of-the-line equipment only to achieve poor results due to basic acoustic issues? Their experience perfectly illustrates the central message of this chapter: understanding and implementing fundamental principles is more important than acquiring expensive gear. A $30 carpet remnant and strategic furniture placement ultimately proved more valuable than thousands of dollars worth of professional equipment.

The key principles we've covered - from microphone selection and room acoustics to recording software and backup systems - form the technical foundation upon which you'll build your podcast. These aren't just theoretical concepts; they're practical tools that will help you create consistent, professional-quality content that keeps listeners engaged.

As you move forward with your podcast, remember that technical excellence doesn't happen overnight. Start with the basics, focus on mastering your initial setup, and make strategic upgrades as your needs evolve. Whether you're starting with a basic USB microphone or investing in professional-grade equipment, the principles we've discussed will help you make informed decisions that support your podcast's growth.

In the next chapter, we'll build upon these technical foundations as we explore content creation and developing your unique podcast voice. The equipment and setup knowledge you've gained here will free you to focus on what truly matters - creating compelling content that resonates with your audience.

3. Content Creation Mastery: Developing Your Unique Voice and Strategy

Every successful podcast begins with a distinctive voice that sets it apart from the millions of other shows competing for listeners' attention. Finding your authentic voice isn't about mimicking popular hosts or forcing a persona - it's about understanding your unique perspective and learning how to share it effectively with your audience. The journey to discovering your authentic podcast voice begins with understanding that authenticity resonates more powerfully with audiences than any carefully crafted persona ever could. In an age where listeners are bombarded with content, they've developed a keen sense for detecting genuine passion and expertise versus manufactured authority.

During my early days as a marketing consultant, I worked with a client who was struggling to find her podcast voice. She was a brilliant financial advisor with deep expertise, but her initial episodes sounded stiff and rehearsed - like she was reading from a textbook. We spent an afternoon recording her simply talking about why she loved helping people with their finances, capturing her natural enthusiasm and conversational style. The difference was remarkable. When we played back both versions, she couldn't believe they were the same person. The formal, scripted approach had masked her genuine passion and warmth. We used that recording as a benchmark for her natural speaking style, and over time, she developed a signature approach that blended her expertise with authentic storytelling. Within six months, her download numbers tripled, and listeners frequently commented on how they felt like they were getting advice from a knowledgeable friend rather than a distant expert. This experience taught me that finding your podcast voice isn't about creating a new persona - it's about removing the barriers that prevent your authentic self from shining through.

In this chapter, we'll explore the essential elements that make up your unique podcast voice and how to develop a content strategy that amplifies your natural strengths. We'll delve into proven techniques for storytelling that can transform your episodes from simple information delivery into engaging narratives that keep listeners coming back for more. Whether you're just starting your podcasting journey or looking to refine your existing approach, the principles and strategies we'll discuss will help you create content that truly connects with your audience.

Developing your content creation mastery isn't just about speaking into a microphone - it's about understanding how to structure your ideas, plan your content calendar, and maintain consistency while staying true to your vision. The most successful podcasters have learned that authentic voice combined with strategic planning creates a foundation for sustainable growth and audience engagement. Let's begin this journey of discovering your unique voice and building the framework that will support your podcast's success.

Developing Your Authentic Podcast Voice and Personality

Your authentic podcast voice is the cornerstone of creating meaningful connections with your audience. In the early days of podcasting, many hosts attempted to mimic traditional radio personalities - adopting an overly polished, announcer-style delivery that created distance between them and their listeners. Today's successful podcasters understand that authenticity trumps perfection every time.

One of the most common mistakes I see new podcasters make is trying to sound like someone else. They study their favorite hosts and attempt to recreate their style, tone, or personality. While it's natural to be inspired by others, mimicry often comes across as inauthentic and can prevent you from developing your unique voice. Your listeners aren't tuning in to hear an imitation - they're seeking your distinct perspective and personality.

- Start with your natural speaking voice and cadence
- Embrace your unique quirks and speech patterns
- Focus on conversational delivery rather than formal presentation
- Let your genuine enthusiasm for your topic shine through
- Be consistent with your energy level across episodes

During a recent consulting session, I worked with a client who was struggling to find her podcast voice. She kept trying to sound 'more professional' by speaking in a lower register and eliminating her natural tendency to laugh while telling stories. The result was stiff and uncomfortable. We recorded her having a casual conversation about her topic with a friend, and the difference was striking. Her natural voice - higher-pitched, punctuated with genuine laughter, and filled with conversational asides - was far more engaging and relatable.

Developing your authentic voice requires practice and self-reflection. Start by recording yourself having natural conversations about your podcast topic with friends or colleagues. Listen back to these recordings and note when you sound most engaged and natural. What topics make you light up? What speaking patterns emerge when you're fully comfortable? These observations will help you identify your authentic voice.

Remember that your podcast voice will evolve over time. Many successful hosts report that it took them 20-30 episodes to truly feel comfortable behind the microphone. Give yourself permission to grow and refine your delivery while staying true to your core personality. Your audience will appreciate your genuineness and grow with you on this journey.

- Record practice sessions where you discuss your topic casually
- Listen back and identify moments of natural engagement
- Note your authentic reactions and emotional responses
- Document speaking patterns that feel most comfortable
- Track your evolution across episodes

Your personality is your podcast's secret weapon. Whether you're naturally analytical, humorous, empathetic, or direct, these traits should inform how you present your content. A host who's naturally detail-oriented might excel at breaking down complex topics, while someone with a quick wit might effectively use humor to maintain engagement. The key is recognizing and leveraging your natural strengths rather than fighting against them.

In my years of consulting, I've observed that podcasters who embrace their authentic voice typically see stronger audience growth and engagement than those who adopt a manufactured persona. Listeners are remarkably perceptive - they can sense when a host is being genuine versus performing a role. This authenticity builds trust and creates a stronger connection with your audience.

Your voice and personality should also align with your podcast's goals and target audience. If you're creating a show about personal finance, your natural teaching style might need slight adjustments to better serve your listeners' needs. However, these adjustments should enhance rather than mask your authentic voice. Think of it as turning up or down certain aspects of your personality rather than creating an entirely new persona.

Remember, your unique perspective and way of communicating are what will set your podcast apart in an increasingly crowded space. Embrace your authentic voice, refine it through practice and feedback, and let it be the foundation upon which you build your podcast's success.

Content Strategy Framework and Editorial Calendar Planning

A well-structured content strategy and editorial calendar are the foundations of a successful podcast. Without these essential planning tools, even the most engaging hosts can find themselves struggling to maintain consistency and quality. I learned this lesson early in my consulting career when working with a talented podcaster who was creating brilliant but sporadic content. Her show would release three episodes one week, then nothing for a month. Despite having engaging content, she was losing listeners due to inconsistent publishing.

Creating a robust content strategy begins with understanding your core message and target audience. This framework should outline your podcast's main themes, content pillars, and the specific value you provide to listeners. Think of it as your podcast's north star - guiding every decision from topic selection to episode structure.

- Define 3-5 main content pillars that align with your expertise
- Identify your target audience's key pain points and interests
- Establish your unique angle or perspective on these topics
- Create a clear value proposition for your listeners
- Develop episode formats that serve your content goals

When I helped my client develop her content strategy, we started by mapping out her areas of expertise and matching them with her audience's needs. This exercise revealed natural content pillars that could sustain months of episodes while maintaining focus and relevance. The key was finding the sweet spot between her knowledge and her listeners' interests.

Your editorial calendar is the practical implementation of your content strategy. It's not just about scheduling episodes - it's about creating a sustainable rhythm for content creation that prevents burnout while maintaining quality. A well-planned calendar should account for your available time, resources, and energy levels.

I recommend planning your editorial calendar at least three months in advance. This gives you enough runway to develop ideas fully while maintaining flexibility to incorporate timely topics or respond to audience feedback. Start by blocking out major themes or series, then fill in specific episode topics.

- Map out key dates and seasonal topics
- Plan content series or thematic arcs
- Schedule guest interviews well in advance
- Build in buffer time for unexpected delays
- Include time for content batch recording

One effective approach I've found is the 'content batching' method. Rather than creating episodes week by week, dedicate specific days to batch-record multiple episodes. This approach helps maintain consistent quality while reducing the overall time commitment. During my consulting work, I've seen this method transform overwhelmed podcasters into confident, consistent content creators.

Your editorial calendar should also include content repurposing plans. Each episode can spawn multiple pieces of content across different platforms - blog posts, social media updates, newsletters, and more. Planning these elements in advance ensures you're maximizing the value of each episode you create.

Remember to build flexibility into your calendar. While consistency is crucial, your planning shouldn't be so rigid that it can't accommodate emerging opportunities or timely topics. I always advise clients to leave some space in their calendar for bonus episodes or special content that aligns with current events in their niche.

- Schedule regular content planning sessions
- Review and adjust your calendar monthly
- Track performance metrics to inform future planning
- Plan promotional activities alongside content
- Include time for audience engagement and feedback review

The most successful podcasters I've worked with treat their editorial calendar as a living document. They regularly review and adjust their plans based on audience feedback, performance metrics, and their own evolving goals. This iterative approach helps ensure their content remains fresh and relevant while maintaining the structure necessary for consistent production.

Your content strategy and editorial calendar should work together to create a sustainable podcasting rhythm. When properly aligned, these tools transform the overwhelming task of regular content creation into a manageable, systematic process that supports both creativity and consistency. The goal isn't to create a rigid structure that stifles spontaneity, but rather to build a framework that supports your natural creative flow while ensuring reliable content delivery to your audience.

Storytelling Techniques for Engaging Episodes

The art of storytelling has been central to human communication since our earliest days gathering around fires to share experiences and wisdom. In podcasting, effective storytelling transforms simple information into compelling narratives that keep listeners engaged episode after episode. During my consulting work, I've observed that shows incorporating strong storytelling elements consistently outperform those that merely present information, regardless of the podcast's topic or genre.

Early in my career, I worked with a client who hosted a business podcast that was struggling to retain listeners despite having valuable content. Her episodes were information-rich but felt disconnected and dry. We restructured her approach to frame each episode's key points within a narrative arc, using real-world examples and personal experiences to illustrate concepts. The transformation was immediate - listener retention increased by 40% within the first month of implementing these storytelling techniques.

- Start with a hook that captures attention immediately
- Create clear story arcs with beginning, middle, and end
- Use descriptive language to paint pictures in listeners' minds
- Incorporate tension and resolution to maintain interest
- Include relevant personal anecdotes that illustrate key points

The most effective podcast stories follow a classic narrative structure while adapting to the unique aspects of audio storytelling. Unlike written or visual media, audio requires special attention to pacing, vocal dynamics, and sound design to create immersive experiences. Your voice becomes the camera, guiding listeners through scenes and emotions.

One particularly effective technique I've found is the 'story stack' method, where you layer multiple narrative threads throughout an episode. For example, you might begin with a personal anecdote, weave in a listener's experience, and connect both to your episode's main topic. This creates depth and resonance while maintaining engagement throughout longer episodes.

Consider the emotional journey you want your listeners to experience. Every story should evoke some form of emotional response - whether it's curiosity, empathy, excitement, or understanding. These emotional connections make your content more memorable and shareable.

- Identify the emotional core of your story
- Create relatable characters or situations
- Build tension through pacing and revelation
- Use silence strategically for impact
- Conclude with clear takeaways or calls to action

Sound design plays a crucial role in podcast storytelling. While you don't need elaborate production, thoughtful use of music, ambient sound, or even simple silence can dramatically enhance your narrative's impact. I often advise clients to think of sound elements as punctuation marks in their audio stories - they help guide listeners through emotional beats and transitions.

Remember that authenticity remains crucial even in crafted narratives. Your stories should feel natural and aligned with your podcast's voice and purpose. One client struggled with this balance until we developed what I call the 'coffee shop test' - if you wouldn't tell this story to a friend over coffee, it probably needs refinement for your podcast.

Effective storytelling also requires practice and refinement. I encourage podcasters to record practice versions of their stories, focusing on different elements each time - pacing in one take, emotional expression in another, vocal variety in a third. This iterative approach helps develop natural storytelling abilities while maintaining authenticity.

- Practice telling stories without scripts
- Record multiple versions with different emphasis
- Listen critically to your delivery and timing
- Get feedback from trusted listeners
- Refine based on audience response

The most powerful podcast stories often come from personal experience or direct observation. While research and second-hand accounts have their place, nothing connects with listeners quite like authentic, first-hand narratives. These stories create bonds of trust and understanding between host and audience that strengthen with each episode.

Your storytelling approach should evolve with your podcast. As you develop your voice and better understand your audience, you'll discover which types of stories resonate most strongly. Pay attention to listener feedback and engagement metrics to refine your narrative techniques over time. The goal is to create stories that not only entertain but also serve your podcast's broader purpose and mission.

Interview Preparation and Guest Management

Successful interview-based podcasts rely as much on thorough preparation and guest management as they do on the actual conversation. Throughout my consulting career, I've seen countless podcasters focus solely on their questions while neglecting the crucial pre-interview groundwork that sets the stage for engaging discussions. The art of interviewing extends far beyond the microphone - it begins weeks before your guest arrives and continues well after the recording ends.

When I first started advising podcast clients, I worked with a host who was struggling to get the most from her expert guests. Despite booking impressive individuals in her field, the conversations felt surface-level and disjointed. We developed a comprehensive pre-interview system that transformed her show. The key was creating a structured approach to guest research and preparation while maintaining enough flexibility for organic conversation.

- Research your guest's background thoroughly
- Review their recent work, publications, or projects
- Identify unique angles or unexplored topics
- Prepare a flexible question framework
- Plan your episode's narrative arc

Pre-interview communication is crucial for setting expectations and ensuring both host and guest are aligned on the episode's goals. Create a simple but comprehensive guest information packet that outlines technical requirements, recording procedures, and content guidelines. This professional touch not only helps guests prepare but also demonstrates your commitment to quality.

One of the most effective techniques I've found is the pre-interview questionnaire. This brief document helps you understand your guest's expertise, preferred topics, and any subjects they'd rather avoid. It also provides valuable information for crafting unique angles that differentiate your interview from others they've done.

- Send clear recording instructions and requirements
- Provide episode format and timing details
- Request bio and headshot in advance
- Confirm technical setup and testing time
- Share your audience demographics and expectations

During my consulting work, I developed what I call the '15-5-1' preparation method. Spend 15 minutes researching your guest's general background, 5 minutes reviewing their recent activities or projects, and 1 minute scanning their social media for current updates. This layered approach ensures you have both depth and recency in your knowledge while maintaining efficiency in your preparation process.

The actual interview management requires its own set of skills and strategies. Start with a pre-recording chat to help your guest feel comfortable and establish rapport. This informal conversation often reveals interesting topics or angles you can explore during the recorded session. Keep your question framework flexible enough to follow interesting tangents while maintaining overall direction.

- Begin with a brief, casual pre-recording conversation
- Establish clear recording signals and protocols
- Monitor time without being obvious about it
- Take notes for potential follow-up questions
- Watch for signs of guest fatigue or distraction

Post-interview management is equally important for building long-term relationships and creating opportunities for future collaboration. Follow up with your guests promptly, sharing appreciation and any immediate positive feedback. Provide clear information about the episode's release date and how they can help promote it to their audience.

Your role as an interviewer extends beyond just asking questions - you're a curator of conversations, a guide for your audience, and a facilitator for your guest's expertise. The best interviews feel like natural conversations while actually being carefully orchestrated experiences that serve both the listener and the guest.

- Send a thank-you note within 24 hours
- Share specific release date and promotion plans
- Provide easy ways for guests to share the episode

- Maintain contact for potential future opportunities
- Request feedback on their experience

Remember that every guest interaction is an opportunity to build your podcast's reputation. Treat each interview as a partnership rather than a transaction. When guests have positive experiences, they're more likely to recommend your show to others in their network, helping you attract more high-quality guests.

The most successful interview-based podcasts I've worked with maintain detailed guest management systems. Create templates for your outreach emails, pre-interview questionnaires, and follow-up communications. This systematized approach ensures consistency while saving time and mental energy for the creative aspects of interviewing.

Your interview preparation and guest management processes should evolve based on experience and feedback. Regular review and refinement of these systems help maintain professional standards while improving efficiency. The goal is to create a smooth, professional experience that serves your audience while respecting and showcasing your guests' expertise.

Content Batch Production and Quality Control

Efficient content production is the cornerstone of sustainable podcasting success. Through my consulting work, I've found that batch production - creating multiple episodes in a single session - is one of the most effective ways to maintain consistent quality while managing your time and energy. This approach transforms sporadic content creation into a streamlined system that serves both creator and audience.

Early in my consulting career, I worked with a podcaster who was struggling to maintain her weekly release schedule. She would record each episode the night before release, often staying up late to edit and publish. The stress affected her performance and content quality. We implemented a batch production system where she recorded four episodes in one focused day, then spent another day editing them all. The transformation was remarkable - not only did her stress levels decrease, but her content quality improved significantly due to the focused approach.

- Schedule dedicated recording days for multiple episodes
- Create a consistent pre-recording routine
- Maintain detailed episode notes and outlines
- Track recording time and energy levels
- Build in breaks between recording sessions

Quality control in batch production requires systematic attention to detail. Develop a pre-recording checklist that covers everything from equipment setup to content preparation. This ensures consistency across episodes while preventing technical issues that could derail your recording session.

The key to successful batch production lies in understanding your personal energy patterns and creative peaks. Some hosts I've worked with are most energetic in the morning, while others hit their stride in the afternoon. Schedule your recording sessions during your peak performance times to maintain consistency across episodes.

- Test all equipment before beginning the session
- Review outlines and notes for all planned episodes
- Keep water and throat lozenges readily available
- Monitor audio levels throughout recording
- Document any technical issues or content concerns

Quality control extends beyond the recording phase. Establish a systematic review process for your batch-produced content. Listen to episodes with specific focus areas in mind - content flow in one pass, audio quality in another, and overall engagement in a third. This layered approach helps catch issues that might be missed in a single review.

During my years of consulting, I've developed what I call the '3-2-1 Quality Control Method.' Review each episode three days after recording for content, two days later for technical quality, and one final time the day before release for overall polish. This spacing allows you to approach each review with fresh ears and perspective.

Your batch production system should include clear organization and file management protocols. Name files consistently, maintain detailed episode notes, and create backup systems that protect your work. I once had a client lose an entire batch of episodes due to poor file management - an experience that led to developing robust organizational systems for all my clients.

- Create standardized file naming conventions
- Maintain detailed episode logs and notes
- Implement multiple backup solutions
- Track editing changes and versions
- Document technical settings and preferences

Remember that batch production doesn't mean sacrificing spontaneity or authenticity. Instead, it provides a framework that allows you to focus fully on content creation without the pressure of looming deadlines. Many of my most successful clients find they're actually more creative and engaging when working within a well-structured batch production system.

Quality control in batch production also means monitoring your own performance throughout the recording session. Pay attention to signs of vocal fatigue or energy drops. Schedule breaks between episodes and maintain good vocal health practices. Your voice is your primary tool - protecting it should be a key component of your production system.

The most effective batch production systems evolve over time. Regular review and refinement of your processes help identify bottlenecks and opportunities for improvement.

Keep detailed notes about what works and what doesn't in your recording sessions. This documentation becomes invaluable as you scale your podcast production.

- Monitor voice quality and energy levels
- Schedule regular system review sessions
- Document successful recording techniques
- Track time spent on different production phases
- Gather feedback from your production team if applicable

Your quality control standards should be clearly documented and consistently applied. Create a production manual that outlines your technical specifications, content guidelines, and review processes. This documentation ensures consistency even when working with others or returning to production after a break.

The goal of batch production and quality control isn't just efficiency - it's creating a sustainable system that consistently delivers value to your audience while protecting your time and energy as a creator. When properly implemented, these systems form the foundation of a successful, long-term podcasting career.

Audience Feedback Integration and Content Iteration

Creating a successful podcast isn't a one-way street - it's an ongoing dialogue with your audience that shapes and refines your content over time. Through my years of consulting, I've witnessed how the most successful podcasts evolve through deliberate audience feedback integration and systematic content iteration. This process transforms casual listeners into engaged community members while continuously improving your show's quality and relevance.

One of my earliest consulting experiences involved working with a podcast that had strong initial growth but began losing listeners after six months. Upon investigation, we discovered they weren't effectively collecting or implementing audience feedback. The host was creating content in isolation, missing valuable insights from their listeners. We implemented a structured feedback system, and within three months, their engagement metrics showed significant improvement.

- Create multiple feedback channels (email, social media, surveys)
- Monitor comments and discussions across platforms
- Track common questions and topic requests
- Analyze episode performance metrics
- Document listener suggestions and critiques

The key to effective feedback integration lies in creating systematic ways to collect, analyze, and implement listener input. Develop clear processes for gathering feedback and establish regular review periods to assess and act on the information you receive. This structured approach ensures that audience insights consistently inform your content decisions.

During my consulting work, I've developed what I call the 'Feedback Loop Framework' - a systematic approach to gathering and implementing audience input. Start by establishing baseline metrics for your show, then regularly collect both quantitative data (download numbers, episode completion rates) and qualitative feedback (listener comments, social media interactions). Review this information monthly to identify trends and opportunities for improvement.

Your content iteration process should be both responsive and strategic. While it's important to address audience feedback, maintain a balance between listener requests and your show's core mission. Not every suggestion needs to be implemented, but each should be considered within the context of your podcast's goals and vision.

- Review feedback on a regular schedule
- Identify patterns in listener responses
- Test new content formats based on feedback
- Measure the impact of implemented changes
- Communicate changes to your audience

One particularly effective technique I've found is the 'pilot episode' approach. When testing new content formats or topics suggested by listeners, create a single episode in the new style and explicitly ask for feedback. This allows you to experiment while maintaining transparency with your audience about the iteration process.

Remember that feedback comes in many forms. Beyond direct comments, pay attention to episode completion rates, social media shares, and changes in subscriber numbers. These metrics can provide valuable insights into how your content resonates with listeners. During my consulting career, I've helped podcasters develop comprehensive feedback tracking systems that combine these various data points into actionable insights.

The iteration process should be visible to your audience. When you make changes based on their feedback, acknowledge their role in shaping the show's evolution. This transparency builds trust and encourages continued engagement. I've seen podcasts transform their most active listeners into passionate advocates simply by demonstrating that their input matters.

- Acknowledge listener contributions
- Share the reasoning behind major changes
- Celebrate successful iterations
- Keep your audience involved in the evolution
- Document your show's transformation

Content iteration isn't just about making changes - it's about making informed improvements that serve both your audience and your podcast's mission. Establish clear criteria for evaluating potential changes, and always test new elements before fully implementing them. This methodical approach helps ensure that your show evolves in a sustainable and meaningful way.

Your feedback integration system should grow with your podcast. As your audience expands, you'll need more sophisticated ways to collect and analyze listener input. Consider using survey tools, creating focus groups, or implementing automated feedback collection systems. The goal is to maintain meaningful connections with your audience even as it grows larger.

Remember that iteration is an ongoing process, not a one-time event. Successful podcasts continuously evolve, responding to changing listener needs and industry trends while maintaining their core identity. Through careful feedback integration and thoughtful iteration, your podcast can build stronger connections with your audience while consistently improving its content quality and relevance.Content creation mastery is the foundation upon which successful podcasts are built. As we've explored throughout this chapter, developing your authentic voice, implementing strategic content planning, and mastering storytelling techniques are essential elements that transform good podcasts into great ones. Initially, podcast creators were limited by both technology and convention, often mimicking traditional radio formats. Today, the medium has evolved to embrace authenticity and personal connection, allowing creators to forge deeper relationships with their audiences through genuine expression and strategic content delivery.

My journey helping podcasters develop their content strategy has taught me that success lies not in perfection, but in consistency and authenticity. The financial advisor who transformed her show by embracing her natural enthusiasm rather than maintaining a formal persona is just one example of how authenticity drives engagement. Her story, like many others I've encountered, demonstrates that listeners connect most strongly with hosts who present their expertise through genuine, relatable communication.

The frameworks and strategies we've covered - from developing your unique voice to implementing batch production systems - provide the structure needed to create sustainable content while maintaining creative freedom. Remember that these tools are meant to support your natural creativity, not restrict it. As you move forward with your podcast, focus on balancing authentic expression with strategic planning.

Whether you're just starting your podcasting journey or looking to refine your existing show, remember that content mastery is an evolving process. The most successful podcasters continuously refine their approach, integrating audience feedback while staying true to their core message. Your authentic voice, combined with strategic content planning and effective storytelling, creates the foundation for meaningful connections with your listeners.

As you implement the techniques and strategies from this chapter, remember that every great podcast starts with a clear vision and develops through consistent practice. Your unique perspective and experiences are your greatest assets - use them to create content that resonates with your audience while staying true to your authentic voice. The path to content mastery is ongoing, but with these tools and frameworks, you're well-equipped to create engaging, sustainable podcast content that serves both you and your listeners.

4. Professional Production: Recording, Editing, and Sound Design Excellence

The magic of a truly professional podcast happens in the intricate dance between recording, editing, and sound design - three distinct but interconnected elements that work together to create an immersive listening experience. While many podcasters focus solely on recording quality, it's the masterful combination of all three elements that separates amateur productions from professional-grade content that keeps listeners coming back for more. The journey from raw recording to polished production involves mastering multiple technical elements that work in harmony to create an engaging listening experience. Think of podcast production like cooking a gourmet meal - while the ingredients (your content) matter tremendously, it's the preparation techniques and presentation that elevate the final dish from good to exceptional.

During a consulting session with a client who produced a weekly interview show, I encountered a common but challenging situation. Their recordings were technically sound, but the final product lacked the professional polish they desired. We discovered they were rushing through post-production, treating editing as simply cutting out mistakes and adding intro music. I spent an afternoon showing them how to develop a proper editing workflow, including techniques for pacing, breathing room, and strategic use of ambient sound. We created a template for their audio processing chain and developed a systematic approach to sound design. The transformation was remarkable - their next episode received immediate listener feedback about the improved audio quality and overall listening experience. This experience reinforced my belief that professional-quality podcast production isn't about having expensive equipment or complex techniques - it's about understanding and implementing fundamental principles consistently. The client's success came from learning to treat each phase of production with equal importance and attention to detail, rather than rushing to publish.

In this chapter, we'll explore the essential elements of professional podcast production - from advanced recording techniques to sophisticated editing workflows and sound design principles. You'll learn how to create a consistent, high-quality sound that keeps listeners engaged and coming back for more. Whether you're recording in a home studio or professional space, these techniques will help you achieve the polished, professional sound that distinguishes successful podcasts from amateur productions.

The art of podcast production has evolved significantly since the early days of basic voice recordings and simple edits. Today's listeners expect crystal-clear audio, seamless editing, and thoughtful sound design that enhances rather than distracts from the content. However, achieving this level of quality doesn't require expensive equipment or years of audio engineering experience - it requires understanding and consistently applying fundamental production principles.

Advanced Microphone Techniques and Room Acoustics

One of my earliest podcast consulting experiences taught me a valuable lesson about microphone technique and room acoustics. A client had invested in a top-of-the-line microphone but was recording in their home office, which had bare walls and hardwood floors. Despite the expensive equipment, their recordings sounded hollow and unprofessional. After implementing some basic acoustic treatments - strategically placed soft furnishings and a few well-positioned acoustic panels - the improvement was dramatic. This experience highlighted how even the best microphone can't overcome poor room acoustics.

Understanding microphone technique starts with knowing your microphone's polar pattern - the three-dimensional space around the microphone where it's most sensitive to sound. The most common patterns for podcasting are cardioid (heart-shaped, picking up sound primarily from the front) and omnidirectional (picking up sound from all directions). For most solo podcasters, a cardioid pattern is ideal as it helps reject unwanted room noise and focuses on your voice.

The distance between you and your microphone, known as proximity effect, significantly impacts your sound quality. As a general rule, maintain a consistent distance of 6-8 inches from the microphone, speaking directly into it at a slight angle to minimize plosives (those popping 'p' and 'b' sounds). If you're using a pop filter - which I highly recommend - you can position yourself slightly closer.

- Key microphone positioning tips:
- Speak across the microphone at a 45-degree angle to reduce plosives
- Maintain consistent distance throughout recording
- Use a microphone stand to prevent handling noise
- Position the microphone at mouth level, angled slightly upward

Room acoustics play an equally crucial role in achieving professional sound quality. Every room has its own acoustic signature based on its size, shape, and the materials within it. Hard, flat surfaces like bare walls and windows reflect sound, creating unwanted echoes and reverberations that can make your recordings sound amateur.

Here are my tried-and-tested room treatment strategies:

- Add soft furnishings like curtains, carpets, or rugs to absorb reflections
- Position acoustic panels at key reflection points
- Use a reflection filter behind your microphone
- Record in smaller spaces when possible
- Avoid rooms with parallel walls if you can

I once worked with a podcaster who transformed her spare bedroom into a recording space using nothing but strategically placed furniture and some DIY acoustic panels. She positioned her desk in a corner, hung heavy curtains over the windows, laid down a thick area rug, and placed a bookshelf along one wall. The improvement in sound quality was remarkable, and the entire setup cost less than a single high-end microphone.

Remember that perfect acoustics aren't always necessary - or even desirable - for every type of podcast. Interview shows might benefit from a slightly 'live' room sound that feels more natural and conversational, while narrative podcasts often need a very 'dry' sound for clarity and intimacy. The key is understanding how your room affects your sound and making intentional choices about your recording environment.

When testing your room acoustics, try this simple exercise: record yourself clapping once loudly, then listen back. If you hear a distinct echo or 'ring' after the clap, your room needs acoustic treatment. Focus first on treating the reflection points directly behind and to the sides of your microphone position.

The combination of proper microphone technique and room acoustics creates the foundation for professional-quality audio. These elements work together to capture your voice clearly and naturally, allowing your content to shine without technical distractions. As you develop your podcast, remember that small adjustments in microphone positioning and room treatment can often make a bigger difference than investing in expensive equipment.

Multi-track Recording and Session Management

Multi-track recording revolutionized the podcasting landscape by enabling hosts to capture and edit multiple audio sources independently. I learned this firsthand when helping a client transition from basic single-track recording to a multi-track workflow. Their interview podcast suddenly gained new life - they could adjust guest volumes separately from the host, remove cross-talk seamlessly, and create a more polished final product. The transformation in their show's quality was immediate and dramatic.

At its core, multi-track recording means capturing different audio sources (like multiple microphones or remote guests) on separate tracks rather than mixing them together during recording. Think of it like cooking - when you keep ingredients separate until the final combination, you have much more control over the end result. This approach gives you maximum flexibility during editing and ensures the highest possible audio quality for each element of your show.

The key to successful multi-track recording lies in proper session management. This means organizing your recording sessions in a way that makes post-production efficient and error-free. I recommend creating a consistent track layout that you use for every episode. For example:

- Track 1: Host microphone
- Track 2: Guest microphone or remote audio
- Track 3: Sound effects/transitions
- Track 4: Background music
- Track 5: Ambient sound/room tone

When I first started consulting, I worked with a podcast host who was struggling to manage complex interview episodes with multiple guests. We developed a color-coding system for their tracks and created templates for different episode formats. This simple organization system cut their editing time in half and significantly reduced technical errors.

Session management extends beyond track organization to include proper file naming conventions, backup procedures, and project templates. I recommend creating a standardized naming structure for all your session files. For example: ShowName *EpisodeNumber* Date_Version. This might seem like a small detail, but when you're managing multiple episodes in production, clear organization becomes crucial.

One of the most powerful aspects of multi-track recording is the ability to apply different processing to different audio sources. Your guest's audio might need more noise reduction while your host microphone requires subtle compression. Working with separate tracks allows you to optimize each audio source independently without affecting the others.

Here are essential best practices for multi-track recording:

- Always record a safety track at a lower level (-12dB) for backup
- Use track markers to note important moments during recording
- Keep a session log for tracking technical issues or editing notes
- Maintain consistent input levels across all microphones
- Record room tone on a separate track for natural-sounding edits

When setting up your multi-track session, consider your signal flow carefully. Each input should be properly gained and monitored before recording begins. I always recommend doing a brief test recording and listening back through headphones to verify all tracks are being captured correctly. This simple step has saved countless recording sessions from technical disasters.

The transition to multi-track recording might seem daunting at first, but the benefits far outweigh the learning curve. The flexibility and control it provides are essential for creating professional-quality podcasts. I've seen shows transform from amateur-sounding productions to polished, professional broadcasts simply by implementing proper multi-track workflows.

Remember that successful multi-track recording isn't just about technical setup - it's about developing a systematic approach to session management that works for your specific needs. Start with basic templates and workflows, then refine them as you become more comfortable with the process. The goal is to create a system that becomes second nature, allowing you to focus on content creation rather than technical details.

One particularly effective approach I've developed with clients is the creation of session checklists. These simple documents outline every step of the recording process, from initial setup to final backup. This ensures consistency across episodes and helps prevent technical oversights, especially when working with guest hosts or production assistants.

Professional Editing Workflows and Best Practices

Early in my consulting career, I worked with a talented podcaster who spent countless hours editing each episode, yet struggled to maintain consistent quality and timely releases. Her process was chaotic - she would jump between different sections, repeatedly revisit the same segments, and often lose track of her progress. Together, we developed a structured editing workflow that transformed her production process, cutting editing time by 60% while improving the final product. This experience taught me that efficient editing isn't about working faster - it's about working smarter through organized, systematic approaches.

Professional podcast editing is much like assembling a puzzle - you need a clear picture of the final product and a methodical approach to putting the pieces together. The key is developing a repeatable workflow that ensures consistency while maintaining creative flexibility. Let's explore the essential elements of a professional editing workflow that will help you create polished episodes efficiently.

The foundation of professional editing begins with proper organization. Before you even open your editing software, create a standardized folder structure for each episode:

- Raw audio files
- Edit session files
- Production notes and scripts
- Final mixes
- Episode assets (music, sound effects, etc.)

This organization system becomes your roadmap through the editing process, ensuring you can easily locate and manage all episode components. I recommend using consistent naming conventions that include episode numbers, dates, and version numbers to track your progress.

A professional editing workflow typically follows these key stages:

- Initial content edit (removing mistakes and unnecessary content)
- Structural edit (arranging segments and improving flow)
- Fine-tuning (adjusting pacing and transitions)
- Sound design integration
- Final mix and mastering

Each stage should be completed sequentially, resisting the urge to jump between different phases. This methodical approach helps maintain focus and ensures nothing gets overlooked. During my years of consulting, I've found that podcasters who stick to this structured approach consistently produce higher-quality episodes in less time.

One of the most valuable editing practices I've developed is the 'first pass' rule. During your initial content edit, focus solely on removing obvious mistakes, long pauses, and unnecessary content. Don't get caught up in fine-tuning or sound design at this stage. This approach helps maintain momentum and prevents the perfectionism that can lead to editing paralysis.

Here are essential best practices for professional editing:

- Always edit with headphones to catch subtle audio issues
- Use keyboard shortcuts to increase editing efficiency
- Create templates for common editing tasks
- Maintain an edit decision list (EDL) for complex episodes
- Save versions at key editing stages for backup

When approaching the structural edit phase, think like a storyteller. This is where you arrange your content for maximum impact and engagement. Pay attention to pacing - varying the rhythm between segments helps maintain listener interest. I often recommend creating a visual outline of your episode structure using markers or labels in your editing software.

The fine-tuning phase is where your podcast truly becomes professional. Focus on:

- Consistent volume levels throughout
- Natural-sounding transitions
- Appropriate pause lengths
- Cross-fade optimization
- Breath control and pacing

Remember that editing is both technical and creative. While following a structured workflow is important, don't let it stifle your creative instincts. Some of the most engaging podcast moments come from unexpected editing choices that serve the story or conversation.

One particularly effective technique I've developed is the 'fresh ears' approach. After completing your edit, step away from it for at least a few hours, preferably overnight. When you return, listen to the entire episode without making any edits, taking notes on areas that need attention. This perspective shift often reveals issues or opportunities you might have missed while deep in the editing process.

Quality control is crucial in professional editing. Develop a final checklist that includes:

- Volume consistency check
- Transition smoothness
- Audio artifact scan
- Intro/outro alignment
- Show notes accuracy
- Metadata verification

Finally, establish a clear backup strategy for your editing projects. I recommend keeping at least three versions of your edit: the initial assembly, a mid-point version, and your final mix. This provides safety nets at crucial stages and allows you to return to previous versions if needed.

Remember that developing an efficient editing workflow takes time and practice. Start with these fundamental principles and adapt them to your specific needs and style. The goal is to create a system that becomes second nature, allowing you to focus on crafting engaging content rather than getting bogged down in technical details.

Sound Design Elements and Music Integration

Sound design and music integration are what transform a basic podcast into an immersive audio experience. Early in my consulting career, I worked with a client who initially viewed music as merely bookends for their show - a quick intro and outro with nothing in between. After helping them develop a more sophisticated approach to sound design, incorporating subtle ambient tracks and strategic music cues, their listener engagement increased dramatically. Listeners commented that the show felt more professional and engaging, demonstrating how thoughtful sound design can elevate content without overshadowing it.

The key to effective podcast sound design lies in understanding its three primary functions: establishing identity, enhancing emotional impact, and improving narrative flow. Your sound design elements - from your theme music to transition effects - should work together to create a consistent audio brand that listeners instantly recognize. Think of these elements as your podcast's visual identity for the ears.

When selecting music and sound elements, consider these essential factors:

- Emotional resonance with your content
- Consistency with your show's tone and brand
- Technical quality and clarity
- Proper licensing and usage rights
- Integration potential with your existing workflow

Creating a sound design template for your show ensures consistency across episodes while saving valuable production time. I recommend developing a core sound palette - a collection of music beds, transitions, and effects that you can use repeatedly. This doesn't mean every episode sounds identical, but rather that there's a familiar audio framework supporting your content.

One of the most common mistakes I see podcasters make is overusing sound design elements. Remember that every sound effect, music cue, or transition should serve a specific purpose. Unnecessary audio elements can distract from your content rather than enhance it. I often advise clients to follow the 'less is more' principle - use sound design elements strategically to punctuate key moments or guide listeners through transitions.

Music integration requires particular attention to both technical and creative aspects. When working with background music (often called 'beds'), pay careful attention to:

- Volume levels that support rather than compete with speech
- Appropriate frequency content that doesn't mask voices
- Musical phrases that complement your content pacing
- Clean entry and exit points for smooth transitions

The technical aspects of sound design require careful consideration of your mix. Background music should typically sit 12-20 dB below your voice levels, depending on the style and energy of the track. Use automation to adjust music levels dynamically, bringing them up during transitions and down during speech.

Here's my recommended approach to building a basic sound design framework:

- Create a signature theme that reflects your show's personality
- Develop standard transition elements for segment changes
- Establish consistent sound treatments for recurring segments
- Build a library of backup music beds for different moods
- Design subtle audio cues for important moments

When implementing sound design elements, timing is crucial. Music transitions should feel natural, not abrupt. I teach clients to use music changes to signal new segments or shifts in tone, much like scene changes in a film. This helps listeners subconsciously understand the structure of your show.

Remember that sound design isn't just about adding music and effects - it's also about using silence effectively. Strategic pauses and moments of quiet can be powerful tools for emphasis or emotional impact. The space between sounds is just as important as the sounds themselves.

A well-designed sound palette should include:

- Main theme music
- Secondary themes for different segments
- Transition effects
- Background ambience options
- Stingers for emphasizing key moments
- Closing theme variations

One particularly effective technique I've developed with clients is creating 'mood boards' for sound design - collections of audio elements grouped by emotional impact or energy level. This makes it easier to maintain consistency while still having flexibility to match your content's emotional needs.

The integration of music and sound design elements should feel organic and intentional. Avoid the temptation to use sound effects or music simply because you have them. Each audio element should enhance your storytelling or help convey information more effectively. When in doubt, ask yourself if removing the element would diminish the listener's experience.

Finally, always ensure you have proper licensing for any music or sound effects you use. The consequences of using copyrighted material without permission can be severe. There are many excellent royalty-free music libraries and sound effect collections available specifically for podcasters. Investing in properly licensed music not only protects your show legally but often provides higher quality options that will enhance your production value.

Audio Processing Chains and Signal Flow

Understanding audio processing chains and signal flow is crucial for achieving professional podcast sound quality. Early in my consulting work, I encountered a client who was frustrated by inconsistent audio quality despite using high-end equipment. The issue wasn't their gear - it was their haphazard approach to signal processing. By implementing a structured processing chain, we transformed their sound from amateur to professional in just one session. This experience taught me that even basic equipment can produce excellent results when the signal flow is properly organized.

An audio processing chain is simply the path your audio signal takes from microphone to final output, including all the processing steps along the way. Think of it like a assembly line for your audio - each stage performs a specific function to enhance the final product. The key is understanding not just what each processor does, but when and where to use it in the chain.

Here's my recommended basic processing chain for podcast vocals:

- Noise Gate (to remove background noise)
- EQ (to shape the basic tone)
- Compression (to control dynamics)
- De-esser (to tame harsh sibilance)
- Final EQ (for fine-tuning)
- Limiter (to prevent digital clipping)

The order of these processors matters significantly. For example, placing compression before EQ can emphasize unwanted frequencies, while noise reduction after compression might introduce artifacts. Understanding these relationships helps you make informed decisions about your signal flow.

One of the most common mistakes I see podcasters make is over-processing their audio. Remember that each processor in your chain should serve a specific purpose. If you can't hear a clear improvement when bypassing a processor, you probably don't need it. Less is often more when it comes to audio processing.

Let's break down each stage of a typical podcast processing chain:

- The noise gate should be set to open just above your room noise floor
- Initial EQ should focus on removing problematic frequencies
- Compression should be gentle, typically 2:1 or 3:1 ratio
- De-essing should target specific sibilant frequencies
- Final EQ should make subtle enhancements to tone
- Limiting should only catch occasional peaks

Proper gain staging throughout your processing chain is crucial. Each processor should receive an appropriate input level, and you should maintain consistent levels between processors. I recommend keeping your peaks around -12 dB until the final limiting stage. This gives you plenty of headroom to work with while avoiding distortion.

When setting up your processing chain, start with all processors bypassed and add them one at a time. This allows you to hear exactly what each processor is contributing to your sound. Take notes on your settings - understanding why you made specific choices helps you develop consistency across episodes.

Here are key principles for maintaining clean signal flow:

- Monitor levels at each stage of processing
- Use processor bypassing to check effectiveness
- Maintain consistent gain structure
- Document your signal chain and settings
- Regular calibration of monitoring levels

One particularly effective technique I've developed is creating processing chain templates for different recording scenarios. For example, you might have one template for solo episodes, another for interviews, and a third for group discussions. This ensures consistency while allowing flexibility for different content types.

Remember that your processing chain should enhance your natural voice, not completely transform it. The goal is to create a polished, professional sound while maintaining authenticity. If your processed audio doesn't sound natural, you've probably gone too far with your processing.

When troubleshooting audio issues, always start by examining your signal flow. Often, problems that seem complex can be traced back to simple signal routing issues or improper processor ordering. I recommend creating a signal flow diagram for your setup - this visual reference can be invaluable when problems arise.

Finally, regularly review and update your processing chain. As your podcast evolves and your skills improve, you may find better ways to achieve your desired sound. Don't be afraid to experiment, but always keep a backup of your proven settings before making significant changes.

The key to successful audio processing is finding the right balance between technical excellence and practical efficiency. Your processing chain should be comprehensive enough to achieve professional sound quality, but simple enough to maintain consistency across episodes. With proper attention to signal flow and thoughtful processing choices, you can achieve professional-quality audio that engages your listeners and enhances your content.

Quality Control and Final Mix Preparation

Quality control and final mix preparation are crucial steps that often get overlooked in the rush to publish. I learned this lesson early in my consulting career when a client called me in a panic - they had just released an episode with significant audio issues that weren't caught during production. We implemented a comprehensive quality control process, and they never faced similar issues again. This experience taught me that proper QC isn't just about catching mistakes - it's about ensuring consistent quality that keeps listeners engaged.

The final mix stage is your last opportunity to ensure your podcast meets professional standards before release. Think of it like a final inspection of a finished product - every element needs to be checked and verified. I recommend developing a systematic approach to quality control that covers both technical and content aspects of your production.

Here's my essential quality control checklist that I share with clients:

- Volume consistency throughout the episode
- Proper intro and outro placement
- Clear speaker identification
- Clean transitions between segments
- Appropriate music and effect levels
- Overall mix balance
- Metadata accuracy
- File format specifications

When preparing your final mix, always listen through multiple playback systems. What sounds perfect in your studio headphones might reveal issues when played through car speakers or earbuds. I advise clients to check their mixes on at least three different systems:

- Professional headphones
- Computer speakers
- Mobile device

One particularly effective technique I've developed is the 'fresh ears' review. After completing your mix, step away for at least a few hours, then listen to the entire episode without interruption. This break helps you hear your content more objectively and often reveals issues that weren't apparent during the editing process.

Technical specifications for your final mix are crucial for consistent delivery across platforms. Standard podcast specifications include:

- 16-bit/44.1kHz WAV or AIFF for master files
- MP3 format for distribution (minimum 128 kbps)
- -16 LUFS for loudness targeting
- Peak limiting at -1 dBTP
- Proper ID3 tags and metadata

Remember that quality control isn't just about technical perfection - it's about ensuring your content effectively reaches and engages your audience. Pay attention to pacing, energy levels, and overall flow. Does the episode maintain listener interest throughout? Are key messages clear and well-presented?

I once worked with a podcast host who was receiving consistent feedback about audio quality issues despite having excellent equipment. When we implemented a thorough QC process, we discovered that subtle background noise was creeping in during certain segments. By adding background noise checking to their quality control workflow, they were able to identify and address these issues before publication.

Final mix preparation should include:

- Normalizing levels across episodes
- Ensuring consistent EQ balance
- Verifying stereo imaging
- Checking for phase issues
- Confirming proper fade-ins and fade-outs
- Validating all audio transitions

Export multiple versions of your final mix for different purposes:

- Full-quality master file for archives
- Distribution version for podcast platforms
- Backup copy with separate stems
- Preview version for quick reference

One of the most valuable quality control practices I recommend is peer review. Having another set of ears listen to your content can provide invaluable feedback and catch issues you might have missed. This doesn't necessarily require a professional audio engineer - even a trusted friend or colleague can offer useful perspective on how your content comes across to listeners.

Finally, maintain a quality control log for each episode. Document any issues found and how they were resolved. This creates a valuable reference for future productions and helps identify recurring problems that might need systematic solutions. Over time, this documentation will help you refine your production process and maintain consistent quality across all your episodes.

Remember that quality control isn't about achieving perfection - it's about ensuring your content meets professional standards and effectively serves your audience. A systematic approach to quality control and final mix preparation will help you deliver consistent, high-quality episodes that keep listeners engaged and coming back for more.As we conclude this chapter on professional podcast production, it's worth reflecting on how far podcast audio quality has evolved since the early days of the medium. The earliest shows were often recorded on basic computer microphones with minimal editing. The focus was simply on getting content out there. Today, listeners expect and deserve better.

The journey from raw recording to polished production involves mastering multiple technical elements that work together to create an engaging listening experience. Throughout this chapter, we've explored essential aspects of professional podcast production - from advanced microphone techniques and room acoustics to sophisticated editing workflows and sound design principles. We've seen how proper session management, organized editing processes, and thoughtful sound design can transform good content into great listening experiences.

The transformation in podcast production quality I witnessed with my interview show client - going from basic edits to implementing proper workflows and sound design - exemplifies what's possible when you apply professional production principles consistently. Their success wasn't about having expensive equipment or complex techniques - it came from understanding and implementing fundamental principles with care and attention to detail.

Remember that achieving professional-quality audio isn't about perfection - it's about creating a consistent, engaging listening experience that serves your content and respects your audience. Whether you're recording in a home studio or professional space, the techniques and workflows covered in this chapter will help you achieve the polished, professional sound that distinguishes successful podcasts from amateur productions.

As you develop your podcast production skills, focus on building systematic approaches to recording, editing, and sound design. Create templates and checklists that work for your specific needs. Establish consistent workflows that become second nature. Most importantly, remember that every technical decision should serve your content and enhance your listeners' experience.

Quality podcast production is an ongoing journey of learning and refinement. Start with the fundamentals, implement them consistently, and gradually build upon that foundation as your skills and confidence grow. Your listeners will appreciate the professional polish you bring to your content, and you'll find the production process becoming more efficient and enjoyable as you master these techniques.

In the next chapter, we'll explore how to take your polished podcast and build an empire around it through strategic marketing and audience engagement. The professional sound you've learned to create will serve as the foundation for growing your show's reach and impact.

5. Building Your Podcast Empire: Marketing, Growth, and Audience Engagement

In today's crowded podcast landscape, creating great content is just the beginning - strategic marketing and audience engagement are what transform good shows into podcast empires. The path to podcast growth requires a multi-channel approach that combines social media presence, community building, and strategic partnerships with a deep understanding of your target audience's needs and behaviors. The reality is that building a thriving podcast requires more than just hitting the record button and hoping listeners will find you. It demands a carefully orchestrated approach to marketing, community building, and audience engagement that works together to create sustainable growth.

Early in my marketing career, I worked with a podcast client who was struggling to grow beyond their initial hundred listeners despite producing excellent content. Their show about urban gardening had passionate followers but wasn't reaching its potential audience. We analyzed their existing marketing efforts and discovered they were solely relying on social media posts announcing new episodes. Together, we developed a comprehensive growth strategy that included creating shareable gardening infographics, partnering with local nurseries for cross-promotion, and building an email list through a free 'Urban Gardening Starter Guide.' The transformation wasn't immediate, but within six months, their subscriber base grew to over 5,000 listeners. The key lesson wasn't just about implementing multiple marketing channels - it was about creating value in each channel that complemented the podcast content. This experience shaped my approach to podcast marketing, showing that sustainable growth comes from building an ecosystem of content and engagement points around your core show.

In this chapter, we'll explore the proven strategies and tactics that can help you build your own podcast empire. From leveraging social media effectively to creating meaningful community engagement, you'll learn how to develop a multi-channel approach that amplifies your show's reach while staying true to your core message. We'll examine how successful podcasts build loyal audiences through strategic partnerships, email marketing, and targeted content distribution. Most importantly, you'll discover how to measure your growth efforts effectively, ensuring that your marketing initiatives translate into real audience engagement and sustainable expansion.

The podcast landscape has evolved significantly since its inception. What began as a niche medium for tech enthusiasts has transformed into a powerful platform for voices across every conceivable topic and interest. This evolution has created unprecedented opportunities for growth, but it has also increased the importance of standing out in an increasingly crowded space. Understanding how to effectively market and grow your podcast has become just as crucial as creating quality content.

As we delve into the strategies for building your podcast empire, remember that sustainable growth isn't about finding a single magic solution - it's about implementing a comprehensive approach that resonates with your target audience and aligns with your show's unique value proposition. Whether you're just starting out or looking to expand an established show, the principles and strategies in this chapter will help you create a robust foundation for long-term success in the podcasting world.

Social Media Strategy and Content Distribution

Social media has become an indispensable tool for podcast growth and audience engagement. When I first started advising podcasters on social media strategy, many viewed it simply as a place to drop their episode links and move on. However, I quickly learned that successful social media promotion requires a more nuanced and strategic approach that treats each platform as its own unique ecosystem.

Let's start with a fundamental truth: your social media strategy should be built around providing value, not just broadcasting content. Think of each social platform as a distinct channel for connecting with your audience, each with its own language and culture. What works on Instagram may fall flat on Twitter, and content that soars on TikTok might not resonate on LinkedIn.

- Create platform-specific content that aligns with each channel's strengths
- Focus on building relationships, not just promoting episodes
- Develop a consistent posting schedule that maintains engagement
- Use multimedia content to showcase your podcast's personality
- Engage authentically with your audience's comments and messages

One of the most effective approaches I've found is the content multiplication strategy. Take your podcast episodes and break them down into multiple pieces of micro-content. A single hour-long episode can yield dozens of social media posts: quote graphics, short video clips, discussion questions, behind-the-scenes photos, and key takeaways. This approach not only maximizes your content's reach but also provides multiple entry points for potential listeners to discover your show.

The key to effective content distribution lies in understanding the timing and frequency of your posts. Through years of working with podcasters, I've observed that consistency often trumps quantity. It's better to maintain a steady presence with quality content than to overwhelm your followers with a flood of posts followed by long periods of silence. Develop a content calendar that aligns with your episode release schedule and your audience's online habits.

When it comes to specific platforms, each offers unique opportunities for podcast promotion. Instagram's visual nature makes it perfect for sharing eye-catching audiograms and quote cards. Twitter excels at real-time engagement and conversation building around your podcast topics. LinkedIn can be invaluable for business-focused shows looking to connect with professional audiences. TikTok's algorithmic discovery makes it powerful for reaching new listeners through creative, short-form content.

- Utilize platform-specific features like Instagram Stories, Twitter Spaces, and LinkedIn Articles
- Create shareable content that encourages audience interaction
- Leverage hashtags strategically to increase discoverability
- Cross-promote between platforms while maintaining platform-specific approaches
- Track engagement metrics to refine your strategy over time

Remember that social media success isn't just about follower counts - it's about building an engaged community around your podcast. I once worked with a client who had a modest following of 500 Instagram followers but managed to convert 80% of them into podcast listeners through consistent, valuable engagement. They responded to every comment, shared listener stories, and created content that sparked genuine conversations. Their approach proved that authentic engagement often yields better results than chasing viral moments.

Content distribution extends beyond social media as well. Consider developing a comprehensive distribution strategy that includes:

- Email newsletters to nurture direct relationships with listeners
- Blog posts that expand on episode topics
- YouTube channels featuring video versions of episodes
- Medium articles that repurpose podcast content
- Partnerships with complementary content creators

The most successful podcasters I've worked with treat content distribution as an ongoing experiment. They consistently test new approaches, measure results, and adjust their strategy based on what resonates with their audience. This iterative approach allows them to build a robust presence across multiple platforms while maintaining authenticity and providing genuine value to their community.

Remember that building a strong social media presence takes time and patience. Focus on creating genuine connections with your audience rather than chasing quick wins. Your social media channels should feel like natural extensions of your podcast, maintaining the same voice, values, and quality that listeners expect from your show. When done right, social media becomes not just a promotional tool, but a vital part of your podcast's overall experience.

Email Marketing and Newsletter Growth

Email marketing remains one of the most powerful tools in a podcaster's growth arsenal, offering a direct line of communication with your most engaged listeners. Early in my consulting career, I worked with a podcast about vintage motorcycles that struggled to maintain consistent listener engagement between episodes. While they had a modest but dedicated following, they weren't fully capitalizing on their audience's enthusiasm. That changed when we implemented a strategic email marketing approach that transformed their casual listeners into a thriving community.

The power of email marketing lies in its intimacy and control. Unlike social media platforms where algorithms determine who sees your content, email provides direct access to your audience's inbox. This direct connection creates opportunities for deeper engagement and relationship building that can significantly impact your podcast's growth.

- Start with a clear value proposition for subscribers
- Develop a consistent email schedule that complements your podcast
- Segment your list based on listener interests and engagement
- Create exclusive content for email subscribers
- Use automation to nurture new subscribers

When developing your email strategy, consider the journey your listeners take from casual subscribers to engaged community members. I recommend creating a welcome sequence that introduces new subscribers to your podcast's best content, core values, and community opportunities. This initial nurture sequence helps set expectations and demonstrates the value of being on your email list.

One of the most effective approaches I've found is treating your newsletter as a companion piece to your podcast, not just a promotional tool. Share behind-the-scenes insights, expand on episode topics, and provide exclusive resources that enhance the listening experience. This approach transforms your email list from a broadcasting channel into a value-added service for your most dedicated listeners.

- Offer exclusive bonus content or early access to episodes
- Share personal insights and stories not included in the podcast
- Provide resource lists and links mentioned in episodes
- Create subscriber-only Q&A opportunities
- Develop special offers for email subscribers

The technical aspects of email marketing matter as much as the content strategy. Choose an email service provider that offers podcast-specific features like audio embedding and automation capabilities. Pay attention to your email deliverability by maintaining list hygiene and following best practices for subject lines and content formatting.

Tracking and analyzing your email metrics is crucial for optimizing your newsletter's performance. Focus on open rates, click-through rates, and engagement patterns to understand what resonates with your audience. Use this data to refine your content strategy and improve subscriber retention.

Remember that building a successful email list takes time and consistent effort. Start with clear goals for your newsletter and develop content that serves your audience's needs while supporting your podcast's growth objectives. The most successful podcast newsletters I've helped develop found their stride by maintaining a balance between promotional content and valuable insights that enhance the listening experience.

Consider implementing these proven strategies for newsletter growth:

- Create compelling lead magnets specific to your podcast topic
- Use strategic call-to-actions within your episodes
- Leverage your show notes for email capture
- Cross-promote your newsletter on social media platforms
- Partner with complementary newsletters for list growth

The relationship between your podcast and newsletter should be symbiotic, each platform enhancing the other's value. Your newsletter can drive podcast listens while your podcast episodes can grow your email list. This circular relationship creates a powerful growth engine for your show.

One often overlooked aspect of email marketing is the opportunity for direct feedback from your audience. Encourage replies and engagement from your subscribers, and use their input to inform your content decisions. This two-way communication channel can provide valuable insights into your audience's interests and needs, helping you create more targeted and engaging podcast content.

As your email list grows, consider segmenting your subscribers based on their interests and engagement levels. This allows you to deliver more personalized content and offers, improving the overall effectiveness of your email marketing efforts. Remember that a smaller, engaged list is more valuable than a large, unresponsive one.

Cross-Promotion and Strategic Partnerships

Strategic partnerships and cross-promotion represent some of the most powerful growth opportunities in podcasting. Early in my consulting career, I worked with a history podcast that struggled to expand beyond its initial audience. While the content was excellent, they were essentially operating in isolation. We developed a partnership strategy that transformed their reach and ultimately tripled their listener base within six months.

The fundamental principle of podcast cross-promotion is simple: find shows with complementary audiences and create mutually beneficial relationships. However, the execution requires careful planning and authentic alignment. The goal isn't just to swap promotional spots, but to create genuine value for both audiences.

- Identify podcasts with overlapping but non-competing audiences
- Focus on quality of partnerships over quantity
- Create authentic, value-driven collaborative content
- Develop clear agreements and expectations

- Track and measure partnership results

When approaching potential partners, it's essential to lead with value. I always advise my clients to thoroughly research potential partners and develop specific ideas for collaboration before making initial contact. This preparation demonstrates professionalism and increases the likelihood of successful partnerships.

The most effective cross-promotional strategies extend beyond simple ad swaps. Consider creating special collaborative episodes, co-hosted series, or shared content initiatives that genuinely excite both audiences. These deeper collaborations often yield better results than traditional promotional exchanges.

One particularly effective approach I've developed is the 'content bridge' strategy. This involves creating content that naturally connects your show's topic with your partner's focus area. For example, I once helped a gardening podcast partner with a cooking show by creating a series about growing and cooking with fresh herbs. The natural overlap provided value to both audiences while expanding each show's reach.

- Develop joint special episodes or mini-series
- Create shared resources or downloads
- Co-host live events or virtual summits
- Collaborate on social media campaigns
- Share expertise as guest contributors

Strategic partnerships can extend beyond other podcasts as well. Consider building relationships with:

- Industry organizations and associations
- Complementary businesses
- Educational institutions
- Online communities and forums
- Content creators in other mediums

The key to sustainable partnerships is maintaining clear communication and mutual benefit. Establish concrete goals and expectations at the outset, and regularly review the partnership's effectiveness. Document your agreements, even with informal partners, to ensure everyone understands their commitments and responsibilities.

Remember that partnership success often depends on timing and alignment. Not every potential collaboration will be right for your show, and that's okay. Focus on partnerships that authentically serve your audience while supporting your growth objectives. I've seen podcasters damage their credibility by pursuing partnerships that didn't align with their core values or audience interests.

When evaluating potential partnerships, consider these key factors:

- Audience alignment and overlap
- Content quality and production values
- Brand values and messaging consistency
- Partnership goals and expectations
- Resource requirements and commitments

One of the most valuable lessons I've learned about podcast partnerships is the importance of long-term thinking. While one-off promotional swaps can provide short-term benefits, the most successful partnerships I've helped develop were those built on ongoing collaboration and mutual growth.

Tracking and measuring partnership results is crucial for optimizing your collaboration strategy. Develop clear metrics for success and regularly evaluate the impact of your partnerships. This data-driven approach helps identify which types of collaborations work best for your show and audience.

The podcast industry's collaborative nature provides unique opportunities for growth through strategic partnerships. By approaching these opportunities with authenticity, preparation, and clear objectives, you can create powerful alliances that benefit both your show and your partners while providing genuine value to your respective audiences.

Community Building and Listener Engagement

Building a thriving community around your podcast is one of the most rewarding and valuable aspects of podcasting. When I first started consulting with podcasters, many viewed community building as a secondary concern, focusing primarily on content creation and marketing. However, I quickly learned that engaged communities become the driving force behind sustainable podcast growth and listener loyalty.

The foundation of community building lies in creating spaces where your listeners can connect not just with you, but with each other. These connections transform passive listeners into active participants in your podcast's journey. I remember working with a client who hosted a gardening podcast - they were producing excellent content but struggled with listener retention. We discovered that by creating a simple Facebook group where listeners could share their own gardening successes and challenges, engagement skyrocketed. The community began generating its own content, asking questions, and supporting each other's horticultural endeavors.

- Create dedicated spaces for listener interaction
- Encourage and facilitate listener-to-listener connections
- Develop community guidelines and moderation strategies
- Plan regular community events and activities
- Recognize and celebrate community members

The key to successful community building is consistency and authenticity in your engagement efforts. Your role as a podcast host extends beyond content creation to community leadership. This means being present, responsive, and genuinely interested in your listeners' perspectives and experiences.

One effective strategy I've developed is the 'Community Spotlight' approach. This involves regularly featuring listener stories, questions, or achievements in your episodes. This not only provides valuable content but also demonstrates that you value your community's input and experiences. It creates a virtuous cycle where listeners become more engaged because they see their contributions being recognized and appreciated.

- Feature listener questions and stories in episodes
- Create community challenges or projects
- Host virtual or in-person meetups
- Develop member recognition programs
- Foster discussions beyond episode topics

Remember that community building is a long-term investment. The most successful podcast communities I've helped develop didn't happen overnight - they grew organically through consistent nurturing and attention. Start with small, manageable initiatives and expand as your community grows and evolves.

Consider implementing these proven community engagement strategies:

- Regular Q&A sessions or 'Ask Me Anything' episodes
- Community polls for content direction
- Behind-the-scenes content access
- Member-only discussions or events
- Collaborative projects or challenges

The technical aspects of community management are just as important as the engagement strategies. Choose platforms and tools that align with your audience's preferences and make it easy for them to participate. Whether it's a dedicated Discord server, Facebook group, or custom community platform, ensure the technology serves your community's needs rather than creating barriers to engagement.

One of the most valuable lessons I've learned about community building is the importance of establishing clear boundaries and expectations. Create community guidelines that foster positive interactions while protecting members from negative behavior. Your role as a community leader includes maintaining these standards and addressing issues promptly when they arise.

The relationship between your podcast content and community should be symbiotic. Let your community inform your content decisions while using your content to spark community discussions and engagement. This reciprocal relationship creates a more dynamic and engaging podcast experience for everyone involved.

Remember that every community has its own unique culture and dynamics. What works for one podcast community might not work for another. Pay attention to your community's natural patterns of interaction and adapt your engagement strategies accordingly. The goal is to facilitate and enhance these natural connections rather than forcing artificial engagement.

Measuring community health goes beyond simple metrics like member counts or post volumes. Look for indicators of meaningful engagement such as:

- Quality of discussions and interactions
- Member retention rates
- User-generated content
- Peer support activities
- Community-initiated projects

The most successful podcast communities I've helped develop share a common characteristic: they provide value beyond the podcast content itself. They become resources for learning, networking, and personal growth. When your community serves these deeper needs, it becomes an integral part of your listeners' lives rather than just a fan group for your show.

As your community grows, consider developing leadership roles for engaged members. This might include moderators, content contributors, or event organizers. Empowering community members to take ownership of certain aspects of the community not only helps with management but also strengthens their connection to the podcast and fellow listeners.

Analytics and Growth Metrics
Understanding your podcast's performance through analytics and metrics is crucial for sustainable growth. When I first started advising podcasters about analytics, many felt overwhelmed by the data available to them. They were either ignoring their metrics entirely or focusing on vanity metrics that didn't provide actionable insights. Over time, I developed a framework that helps podcasters focus on the metrics that truly matter for their show's growth and success.

The foundation of effective podcast analytics lies in understanding what to measure and why. While download numbers are important, they're just one piece of a larger puzzle that includes listener engagement, retention, and conversion metrics. I remember working with a client who was discouraged by their seemingly modest download numbers until we analyzed their listener retention data. We discovered that while their total audience wasn't huge, over 90% of their listeners were completing each episode - an incredibly valuable metric that spoke to the quality of their content.

- Track download trends and growth patterns
- Monitor listener retention and drop-off points
- Analyze audience demographics and locations

- Measure engagement across platforms
- Track conversion rates from marketing efforts

Understanding your audience's listening patterns can provide invaluable insights for content planning and show development. Pay attention to metrics like average listening duration, episode completion rates, and popular time slots. These data points can help you optimize your content length, release schedule, and episode structure.

One of the most effective approaches I've found is establishing a regular analytics review routine. Set aside time each month to examine your key metrics and look for patterns or trends that can inform your content and marketing strategies. This systematic approach helps you make data-driven decisions while avoiding the trap of obsessing over daily numbers.

The technical aspects of analytics tracking are just as important as the interpretation. Ensure your hosting platform provides comprehensive analytics and consider implementing additional tracking tools for your website and social media presence. This multi-platform approach gives you a complete picture of your podcast's performance and audience behavior.

- Set up proper tracking across all platforms
- Establish baseline metrics for comparison
- Create regular reporting schedules
- Document growth initiatives and their impact
- Monitor competitive benchmarks

Remember that different metrics matter at different stages of your podcast's growth. Early on, focus on engagement metrics that help you understand and serve your core audience. As your show grows, expand your analysis to include broader reach and monetization metrics. The goal is to use data to inform your decisions while staying true to your show's core mission and values.

Consider tracking these key performance indicators:

- Episode download trends
- Listener retention rates
- Geographic distribution
- Device and platform preferences
- Social media engagement
- Website traffic and conversions

One often overlooked aspect of podcast analytics is the importance of qualitative data. While numbers are important, don't forget to track and analyze listener feedback, reviews, and community engagement. These qualitative insights often provide context that helps explain the trends you see in your quantitative metrics.

The relationship between different metrics can reveal important insights about your show's performance. For example, comparing social media engagement metrics with episode downloads can help you understand which promotional strategies are most effective. Similarly, analyzing the correlation between episode topics and listener retention can guide your content planning.

When it comes to growth metrics, focus on sustainable trends rather than short-term spikes. While viral moments can provide temporary boosts, consistent, steady growth often indicates stronger audience connection and more sustainable success. I've seen podcasters become discouraged when they can't maintain viral growth rates, but steady, organic growth usually leads to more engaged and loyal listeners.

Remember that analytics should inform your decisions, not dictate them. Use data as a tool to understand your audience and improve your show, but don't let metrics drive you away from your core mission and authentic voice. Some of the most successful podcasts I've worked with maintained their unique approach while using analytics to optimize their delivery and reach.

The most valuable metrics often vary by podcast genre and goals. A news podcast might focus on daily download numbers and geographic reach, while an educational show might prioritize completion rates and resource downloads. Identify the metrics that align with your specific goals and focus your analysis there.

Finally, don't forget to celebrate your wins, no matter how small they might seem. Every new listener, positive review, or improvement in your metrics represents real progress in building your podcast audience. Track your progress over time and use these achievements to motivate your continued growth and improvement.

Paid Marketing and Advertising Strategies

While organic growth strategies form the foundation of podcast marketing, strategic use of paid advertising can significantly accelerate your show's growth. Early in my consulting career, I worked with a business podcast that was struggling to break through to their target audience despite having excellent content. Through careful implementation of paid marketing strategies, we were able to triple their listener base in just four months while maintaining a positive return on ad spend.

Paid marketing for podcasts requires a thoughtful approach that balances cost with potential return. The key is understanding where your target audience spends their time and how to reach them effectively through paid channels. Let's explore the most effective paid marketing strategies I've developed over two decades of helping podcasters grow their shows.

- Targeted social media advertising
- Podcast directory advertising
- Google Ads and SEO marketing

- Newsletter and email sponsorships
- Influencer partnerships

Social media advertising platforms offer some of the most precise targeting options for podcast promotion. Through years of testing, I've found that the most successful podcast ads on social media focus on specific episode topics or themes rather than general show promotion. This approach allows you to target users based on their interests in those specific topics, increasing the likelihood of connecting with engaged listeners.

One particularly effective strategy I've developed is the 'Content Preview' approach. This involves creating short, engaging video or audio clips from your episodes and using them as ad creative. These previews give potential listeners a taste of your content while demonstrating your show's value proposition. When combined with targeted audience parameters, this approach consistently yields better conversion rates than traditional promotional messaging.

Paid promotion on podcast directories and platforms can also be highly effective when done strategically. Many major podcast platforms offer promotional opportunities, from featured placements to sponsored listings. While these can be more expensive than social media advertising, they often deliver higher-quality listeners who are already active podcast consumers.

- Research platform-specific advertising options
- Test different ad formats and placements
- Monitor and optimize campaign performance
- Focus on ROI rather than just reach
- Develop platform-specific creative assets

Google Ads and SEO marketing represent another valuable channel for podcast growth. While traditional SEO takes time to build, strategic use of Google Ads can help you appear in relevant searches immediately. Focus on keywords related to your podcast topics and target audience interests rather than just podcast-specific terms.

Newsletter and email sponsorships can be particularly effective for reaching engaged audiences. Look for newsletters that serve your target demographic but aren't direct competitors. I've helped clients achieve remarkable success by sponsoring niche newsletters that perfectly aligned with their podcast topics.

When implementing paid marketing strategies, it's crucial to establish clear tracking mechanisms and success metrics. Start with small test budgets and scale up based on performance data. I always advise my clients to set aside 10-15% of their marketing budget for testing new platforms and ad formats.

- Set clear campaign objectives
- Establish tracking mechanisms
- Start with small test budgets

- Scale successful campaigns gradually
- Monitor customer acquisition costs

One often overlooked aspect of paid marketing is the importance of landing page optimization. Whether you're driving traffic to your podcast website or directory listing, ensure your landing page effectively communicates your value proposition and makes it easy for new listeners to start engaging with your content.

Influencer partnerships, while technically paid marketing, require a different approach than traditional advertising. The key is finding influencers whose audiences align naturally with your podcast's focus. I've seen the best results when these partnerships include authentic content integration rather than just promotional mentions.

Remember that paid marketing should complement, not replace, your organic growth strategies. The most successful podcast marketing campaigns I've helped develop integrated paid and organic approaches to create a comprehensive growth strategy. This might mean using paid ads to amplify your best-performing organic content or targeting ads to audiences similar to your most engaged listeners.

When it comes to budget allocation, I recommend starting with a modest monthly investment and scaling based on results. Track your customer acquisition costs carefully and adjust your strategy based on which channels deliver the best return on investment. Don't be afraid to pause campaigns that aren't performing and reallocate those funds to more effective channels.

Finally, remember that paid marketing success often comes down to testing and optimization. What works for one podcast may not work for another, so be prepared to experiment with different approaches while maintaining careful tracking of your results. The goal is to find the combination of paid marketing strategies that works best for your specific show and audience.Building a successful podcast empire isn't just about creating great content - it's about strategically growing and engaging your audience through multiple channels while staying true to your show's core mission. As we've explored throughout this chapter, the landscape of podcast growth has evolved significantly since the medium's early days. What began as a niche technology experiment has transformed into a sophisticated media ecosystem that demands a multi-faceted approach to marketing and audience development.

When I reflect on my journey helping podcasters grow their shows over the past two decades, I'm struck by how the fundamentals of audience building remain constant even as the tools and platforms continue to evolve. The most successful podcasters I've worked with understand that sustainable growth comes from building genuine connections with their listeners while strategically leveraging both organic and paid marketing channels.

The strategies we've covered in this chapter - from social media engagement to email marketing, strategic partnerships to paid advertising - work best when implemented as part of a cohesive growth strategy. Think of these various approaches as instruments in an orchestra. While each can make beautiful music on its own, it's the harmonious combination that creates a truly powerful performance.

Remember that building your podcast empire is a marathon, not a sprint. Focus on creating value for your listeners across every touchpoint, whether that's through engaging social media content, insightful newsletters, or strategic partnerships that enhance your show's value proposition. Track your metrics thoughtfully, but don't let numbers drive you away from your authentic voice and mission.

As you move forward with growing your show, keep in mind that the most valuable asset you can build is a engaged community of listeners who feel genuinely connected to your content and mission. While download numbers and subscriber counts are important metrics, it's the depth of engagement and loyalty from your audience that will sustain your podcast's growth over the long term.

The journey from passionate podcaster to podcast empire builder requires patience, persistence, and strategic thinking. But by implementing the strategies and approaches we've discussed in this chapter, you're well-equipped to build a thriving podcast that resonates with your target audience and achieves sustainable growth.

Now it's time to put these strategies into action. Start by reviewing your current growth initiatives and identifying areas where you can implement or optimize the approaches we've covered. Remember, you don't need to implement everything at once - choose the strategies that align best with your show's goals and audience, then expand your efforts as you see results. Your podcast empire awaits!

6. Monetization Mastery: Multiple Revenue Streams for Podcast Success

The journey from passion project to profitable podcast requires strategic thinking and multiple revenue pathways working in harmony. While many podcasters focus solely on advertising income, the most successful shows typically leverage at least three distinct revenue streams to create sustainable growth and financial stability. The secret to building a sustainable podcast business lies in diversifying your revenue streams while staying true to your core mission and audience trust. In my decades of marketing experience, I've watched countless podcasters struggle by putting all their monetization eggs in one basket - usually advertising - only to find themselves vulnerable to market shifts and audience changes.

In my early days of consulting, I worked with a podcast client who was struggling to monetize their show about personal finance. Despite having a modest but engaged audience of 2,000 listeners, they couldn't secure traditional advertising deals. Instead of giving up, we developed a multi-faceted approach to revenue generation. We created a premium membership tier offering extended episodes and exclusive Q&A sessions, launched a carefully curated selection of branded financial planning templates, and established a monthly workshop series. The transformation was remarkable - within eight months, the show was generating more revenue from these combined sources than they would have made from traditional advertising with ten times their audience size. The key insight wasn't just about diversifying income streams; it was about understanding how different monetization methods could complement each other while adding value for listeners. This experience fundamentally changed how I approach podcast monetization strategy, showing that successful revenue generation isn't just about audience size - it's about creating multiple touchpoints for audience engagement and value delivery.

The podcast monetization landscape has evolved significantly since the medium's early days. What began as a purely advertising-driven model has expanded into a rich ecosystem of revenue opportunities. Today's successful podcasters understand that building a sustainable business requires thinking beyond traditional sponsorship models. Whether you're just starting out or looking to expand your existing revenue streams, this chapter will guide you through proven strategies for turning your podcast into a profitable venture while maintaining the authenticity your audience expects.

As we explore various monetization methods, remember that not every strategy will be right for every show. The key is finding the right mix of revenue streams that align with your content, resonate with your audience, and support your long-term goals. Let's dive into the practical steps and proven approaches that can transform your podcast from a passion project into a profitable business venture.

Sponsorship and Advertising: Strategies and Best Practices
When it comes to podcast monetization, sponsorships and advertising remain the most well-established revenue streams in the industry. As someone who has guided numerous clients through their first sponsorship deals, I can tell you that success in this area requires more than just having a decent listener base - it demands strategic thinking, professional presentation, and a deep understanding of both your audience and potential sponsors' needs.

One of my earliest podcast consulting experiences involved helping a gardening show secure their first sponsor. The host was passionate about organic farming but struggled to attract advertisers despite having a dedicated following. The breakthrough came when we shifted from chasing generic advertisers to targeting businesses that aligned perfectly with their audience's interests and values. By creating a detailed listener demographic profile and crafting a professional media kit that highlighted their audience's purchasing habits, we were able to secure partnerships with organic seed companies and gardening tool manufacturers that proved profitable for both parties.

When approaching sponsorships and advertising, there are several key strategies that consistently prove effective:

- Know Your Numbers: Track and document your download statistics, listener demographics, and engagement metrics
- Create Professional Materials: Develop a comprehensive media kit that includes audience data, show statistics, and value proposition
- Define Your Rate Card: Establish clear pricing for different ad placement options (pre-roll, mid-roll, post-roll)
- Maintain Authenticity: Only partner with brands that align with your show's values and audience interests
- Test and Measure: Track performance metrics for sponsors and be prepared to adjust strategies based on results

The art of integrating sponsorships effectively into your content requires careful consideration. Dynamic ad insertion has become increasingly popular, allowing for more flexible and targeted advertising opportunities. However, many successful podcasters still prefer host-read ads, which tend to perform better due to the trust relationship built with listeners.

One common mistake I've seen podcasters make is undervaluing their audience. Remember, a smaller, highly engaged audience can be more valuable to the right sponsor than a larger but less engaged one. I once worked with a niche technology podcast that had just 5,000 listeners but secured higher sponsorship rates than shows with triple their audience because their listeners were highly qualified decision-makers in the tech industry.

When it comes to ad placement, timing is crucial. While pre-roll ads (at the beginning of episodes) are common, mid-roll placements often command higher rates because listeners are more engaged at that point. Post-roll ads typically have the lowest rates but can be effective for calls-to-action or special offers.

Here are some best practices for implementing ads effectively:

- Keep ad reads natural and conversational
- Integrate sponsorship messages seamlessly into your content flow
- Maintain transparency with your audience about sponsored content
- Provide clear call-to-action instructions and tracking codes
- Regular communication with sponsors about performance and results

Developing long-term relationships with sponsors can lead to more stable revenue streams. I've seen many podcasters evolve from one-off sponsorship deals to ongoing partnerships that include cross-platform promotion, special events, and custom content creation. These deeper relationships often prove more valuable than traditional spot advertising.

Remember that sponsorship success isn't just about landing deals - it's about maintaining professional relationships and delivering value to both sponsors and listeners. Regular reporting, open communication, and a willingness to adapt based on feedback are essential elements of a sustainable sponsorship strategy.

As your show grows, consider developing a diverse sponsor portfolio rather than relying on a single major sponsor. This approach not only provides more stable revenue but also offers listeners variety and reduces dependency on any single advertiser. The key is finding the right balance between monetization and maintaining the authentic connection with your audience that made your show successful in the first place.

Premium Content Models and Subscription Services

Premium content and subscription models represent one of the fastest-growing revenue streams in podcasting. When I first started advising clients about podcast monetization, the idea of listeners paying directly for content seemed far-fetched. However, the landscape has evolved dramatically, with audiences now increasingly willing to support creators directly in exchange for exclusive content and enhanced experiences.

I remember working with a history podcast creator who was hesitant to implement a premium model, worried it would alienate their existing audience. We started small, offering extended episodes and ad-free versions through a basic membership tier. The response surprised us both - within three months, over 15% of their regular listeners had converted to paid subscribers. The key was ensuring the free content remained valuable while offering genuine enhancements for subscribers.

When developing a premium content strategy, consider these proven models:

- Exclusive Extended Episodes: Longer, more detailed versions of regular episodes
- Early Access: Releasing content to subscribers before the general public
- Ad-Free Listening: Clean versions of episodes without sponsorship messages
- Bonus Content: Additional episodes or content not available to free listeners
- Behind-the-Scenes Material: Production insights and extra commentary
- Direct Access: Q&A sessions or community interaction with hosts

The success of your premium model often depends on how you structure and present these offerings. During my consulting work, I've found that a tiered approach typically works best, giving listeners options that match their level of interest and support.

One of the most valuable lessons I've learned about premium content is the importance of consistency and value delivery. A client of mine launched a premium tier offering bonus monthly episodes but struggled to maintain the production schedule. We restructured their workflow to batch-produce premium content, ensuring reliable delivery while maintaining quality. This systematic approach led to higher subscriber retention rates and positive word-of-mouth growth.

When it comes to pricing your premium content, the key is finding the sweet spot between value and accessibility. Through years of testing with various clients, I've observed that starting with a lower-priced tier (around $5-7 monthly) and offering higher-value options can help build a sustainable subscriber base. The goal is to create a clear value proposition that makes the subscription feel like an obvious choice for engaged listeners.

Implementing a premium model requires careful consideration of your platform choice. Popular options like Patreon, Supercast, and Supporting Cast each offer different features and fee structures. The platform you choose should align with your content strategy and audience preferences. I've seen podcasters struggle with platform limitations after growing their subscriber base, so it's important to think about scalability from the start.

Here are essential elements for a successful premium content strategy:

- Clear Value Proposition: Explicitly communicate what subscribers receive
- Consistent Delivery: Maintain a reliable schedule for premium content
- Quality Standards: Ensure premium content matches or exceeds free content quality
- Engagement Focus: Create opportunities for subscriber interaction and feedback
- Regular Evolution: Continuously adapt offerings based on subscriber input

One often overlooked aspect of premium content is the opportunity for community building. A cooking podcast I advised transformed their premium tier into a vibrant community where subscribers shared recipes, participated in monthly cooking challenges, and received personalized feedback from the host. This engagement led to higher retention rates and organic growth through member referrals.

Remember that launching a premium model doesn't mean abandoning or diminishing your free content. The free show remains your primary audience-building tool and should continue to provide substantial value. Think of your premium content as an enhancement rather than a replacement - an opportunity for your most engaged listeners to deepen their connection with your show while supporting its continued growth.

Tracking and analyzing subscriber behavior is crucial for optimizing your premium offerings. Pay attention to which content drives the most conversions, when subscribers tend to cancel, and what feedback they provide. This data helps you refine your premium strategy and ensure you're delivering value that keeps subscribers engaged long-term.

Merchandise Development and E-commerce Integration

Merchandise and e-commerce represent powerful opportunities to both monetize your podcast and deepen listener engagement through tangible brand connections. Early in my consulting career, I worked with a true crime podcast that was hesitant to venture into merchandise, believing their serious subject matter wouldn't translate well to products. We started small with high-quality notebooks featuring their signature tagline and minimalist design. The response was overwhelming - listeners loved having a physical connection to the show they used daily. This experience taught me that merchandise isn't just about selling products; it's about creating touchpoints that strengthen the bond between show and audience.

When developing a merchandise strategy, the key is understanding your audience's lifestyle and how your brand can add value to their daily lives. Consider these fundamental merchandise categories that consistently perform well:

- Wearables: T-shirts, hoodies, and caps with show branding or catchphrases
- Practical Items: Mugs, water bottles, and tote bags
- Stationery: Notebooks, stickers, and planners
- Digital Products: Downloadable resources and templates
- Limited Edition Items: Special releases tied to show milestones or events

The success of podcast merchandise often lies in the authenticity of its connection to your show's brand and message. During my years advising podcasters on merchandise development, I've found that items that reflect the show's core values and inside jokes tend to perform better than generic branded products.

One of the most crucial aspects of merchandise success is quality control. I once helped a client recover from a merchandise disaster where they had rushed to market with low-quality t-shirts that fell apart after a few washes. The experience damaged their brand reputation and taught us valuable lessons about vendor selection and product testing. Now, I always advise podcasters to start with small batch orders and thoroughly test products before large-scale launches.

When it comes to e-commerce integration, selecting the right platform is crucial. Your online store should be easy to manage while providing a smooth shopping experience for customers. Consider these key factors when setting up your e-commerce presence:

- Platform Reliability: Choose established e-commerce solutions with proven track records
- Integration Capabilities: Ensure seamless connection with your existing website and systems
- Inventory Management: Select tools that help track stock levels and automate reorders
- Shipping Solutions: Partner with reliable fulfillment services to handle distribution
- Customer Service: Implement systems to handle inquiries and returns efficiently

Pricing strategy plays a crucial role in merchandise success. Through my consulting work, I've found that podcasters often underprice their merchandise, failing to account for all costs involved. Remember to factor in not just production costs, but also shipping, handling, platform fees, and potential returns when setting your prices.

One effective approach I've seen work well is the launch of seasonal or limited-edition merchandise collections. A cooking podcast I advised created quarterly merchandise releases tied to seasonal themes, generating excitement and urgency among their audience. This strategy not only drove sales but also created regular touchpoints for audience engagement throughout the year.

Here are essential best practices for merchandise development:

- Start Small: Test market demand with a limited product line
- Focus on Quality: Prioritize product durability and customer satisfaction

- Brand Consistency: Ensure merchandise aligns with your show's visual identity
- Listen to Feedback: Incorporate audience suggestions in product development
- Track Performance: Monitor sales data to inform future merchandise decisions

Remember that merchandise success isn't just about sales numbers - it's about creating products that enhance your listeners' connection to your show. The most successful podcast merchandise programs I've helped develop have focused on creating genuine value for their audience rather than just pushing products.

When it comes to fulfillment, consider starting with print-on-demand services before moving to inventory-based models. This approach minimizes upfront costs and risk while allowing you to test different designs and products. As your merchandise line grows, you can transition to bulk ordering for better margins on proven sellers.

Don't overlook the marketing potential of your merchandise. Every item sold becomes a walking advertisement for your show. I've worked with podcasters who've traced new listener growth directly to conversations started by someone wearing their show's merchandise. This organic marketing effect can be particularly powerful when your merchandise designs spark curiosity or conversation.

Crowdfunding and Community Support Systems

Community-driven funding has emerged as one of the most powerful and sustainable ways to monetize podcasting while deepening audience relationships. During my consulting work, I've seen firsthand how crowdfunding can transform a podcast from a passion project into a community-supported media venture. The key lies in understanding that crowdfunding isn't just about collecting donations - it's about building a sustainable support system that benefits both creators and listeners.

Early in my career, I worked with a science education podcast that was struggling to maintain consistent production with limited resources. Rather than pursuing traditional advertising, we developed a community support model that invited listeners to become active stakeholders in the show's future. By offering multiple support tiers with meaningful benefits and regular community engagement opportunities, the podcast built a loyal base of monthly supporters that provided stable funding while creating a vibrant community around the show.

When developing a crowdfunding strategy, consider these proven approaches:

- Monthly Support Tiers: Different levels of recurring support with scaled benefits
- One-Time Contribution Options: Special project funding or equipment upgrades
- Virtual Tip Jar: Easy ways for listeners to show appreciation for specific episodes
- Community Goals: Shared funding targets that unlock new content or features
- Transparency Reports: Regular updates on how community support is used
- Supporter Recognition: Thoughtful ways to acknowledge contributor support

The success of community funding often depends on clear communication about how support directly improves the podcast. I've found that listeners are more likely to contribute when they understand exactly how their support impacts the show's quality and sustainability.

One of the most valuable lessons I've learned about crowdfunding is the importance of building genuine community engagement alongside financial support. A history podcast I advised transformed their Patreon from a simple donation platform into a vibrant community where supporters participated in episode planning, suggested topics, and engaged in meaningful discussions. This level of involvement led to higher retention rates and organic growth through word-of-mouth recommendations.

Platform selection plays a crucial role in crowdfunding success. While Patreon remains popular, platforms like Buy Me a Coffee, Ko-fi, and direct website integration offer different features and fee structures. The key is choosing a platform that aligns with your community's preferences and your administrative capabilities.

Here are essential elements for successful community support systems:

- Clear Value Proposition: Explain how support benefits both the show and community
- Regular Communication: Keep supporters informed and engaged
- Meaningful Rewards: Offer benefits that enhance the listening experience
- Community Input: Create opportunities for supporters to influence content
- Sustainable Goals: Set realistic funding targets that align with show needs

Remember that building community support takes time and consistent effort. Start with modest goals and focus on creating genuine value for supporters. I've seen podcasters rush to launch crowdfunding campaigns without proper planning, leading to disappointing results and damaged listener relationships.

One often overlooked aspect of community support is the power of non-financial contributions. Consider creating opportunities for listeners to support the show through skills, expertise, or volunteer time. A true crime podcast I worked with built a research team from dedicated listeners who helped verify historical details and uncover new information for episodes.

When implementing a community support system, transparency becomes crucial. Regular updates about how funds are used, progress toward goals, and future plans help maintain trust and encourage ongoing support. This openness also creates opportunities for deeper community engagement as supporters feel more connected to the show's development and success.

The most successful community-supported podcasts I've worked with understand that crowdfunding is a two-way relationship. They consistently deliver value to their supporters while remaining open to feedback and adaptation. This approach creates a sustainable cycle where community support enables better content, which in turn attracts more support and engagement.

Consulting and Speaking Opportunities

Your expertise as a podcaster can open doors to valuable consulting and speaking opportunities that extend far beyond your show. Throughout my consulting career, I've watched numerous podcasters transform their show's success into thriving careers as sought-after experts and speakers. The key lies in understanding how to leverage your podcast platform to establish yourself as an authority in your field.

I recall working with a client who hosted a podcast about small business marketing. While her show had modest listenership, she consistently delivered actionable insights that resonated with her audience. We developed a strategy to showcase her expertise through guest appearances on other podcasts and local business events. Within a year, she was earning more from consulting and speaking engagements than from direct podcast monetization. Her journey taught me that the path to consulting success often starts with identifying your unique value proposition and building credibility through consistent content delivery.

When developing your consulting and speaking career, consider these proven approaches:

- Workshop Development: Create practical training sessions based on your podcast expertise
- One-on-One Consulting: Offer personalized guidance in your area of specialization
- Group Coaching Programs: Scale your impact through structured group sessions
- Speaking Engagements: Share your insights at industry events and conferences
- Corporate Training: Develop programs for businesses and organizations

The transition from podcaster to consultant requires careful positioning and professional presentation. During my years advising content creators, I've found that successful podcast consultants focus on solving specific problems rather than offering general advice. This targeted approach helps differentiate your services and justify premium pricing.

One of the most effective ways to launch your consulting practice is by creating a signature framework or methodology based on your podcast content. I worked with a productivity podcast host who distilled their most popular episodes into a structured consulting program. This systematic approach not only made their services more valuable but also more scalable as they could train others to deliver their methodology.

When it comes to speaking opportunities, your podcast provides an excellent platform to demonstrate your presentation skills and thought leadership. Consider these strategies for developing your speaking career:

- Record Speaking Samples: Create highlight reels from your best podcast moments
- Develop Signature Topics: Craft compelling presentations based on popular episodes

- Build a Professional Speaker Kit: Include your podcast metrics and audience demographics
- Network Within Your Niche: Connect with event organizers in your industry
- Start Local: Build experience with smaller, local events before pursuing larger venues

Remember that consulting and speaking success often depends on maintaining high visibility within your industry. Regular podcast content helps keep you top-of-mind with potential clients while demonstrating your ongoing expertise and thought leadership. Your show becomes a powerful marketing tool for your consulting practice, creating a virtuous cycle of content and opportunities.

Pricing your consulting services requires careful consideration of your market position and value delivery. Through my experience guiding podcasters into consulting roles, I've found that many initially undervalue their expertise. Start by researching market rates for similar services in your industry and consider how your unique podcast platform adds value to your offerings.

Here are essential elements for building a successful consulting practice:

- Clear Service Offerings: Define specific packages and deliverables
- Professional Systems: Implement efficient booking and delivery processes
- Results Tracking: Document client successes and testimonials
- Continuous Learning: Stay current with industry trends and developments
- Network Building: Cultivate relationships with other experts and potential clients

One often overlooked aspect of podcast-based consulting is the opportunity to create additional revenue streams through supplementary products and services. A client of mine who hosted a business strategy podcast developed a suite of digital tools and templates that complemented their consulting services, creating passive income alongside their active consulting work.

As you develop your consulting and speaking career, maintain focus on delivering genuine value while staying true to your podcast's core message and audience. The most successful podcast consultants I've worked with view their show and consulting practice as complementary elements of a broader business strategy, each supporting and enhancing the other's growth.

Licensing and Content Syndication

Licensing and content syndication represent increasingly valuable revenue streams in the podcasting ecosystem, offering opportunities to expand your reach while generating additional income from your existing content. Through my years of consulting, I've watched this space evolve from simple RSS feeds to sophisticated distribution networks that can significantly amplify a show's impact and earning potential.

Early in my consulting career, I worked with a podcast focused on workplace productivity that was struggling to grow beyond their core audience. We discovered untapped potential in their extensive episode library. By licensing their content to corporate training programs and syndicating specific episodes to relevant business platforms, they created new revenue streams while reaching previously untapped audiences. This experience taught me that content creators often underestimate the value of their existing library.

When approaching licensing and syndication, consider these proven strategies:

- Content Repackaging: Transform episodes into training materials or educational content
- Platform Partnerships: Negotiate deals with specialized content platforms
- International Rights: License content for translation and distribution in other markets
- Corporate Licensing: Create custom packages for organizational use
- Media Partnerships: Collaborate with traditional media outlets for content sharing

The key to successful licensing lies in understanding the unique value of your content and identifying the right partners for distribution. During my consulting work, I've found that niche content often has more licensing potential than general interest material, particularly when targeting specific industries or use cases.

One of my clients produced a health and wellness podcast that found success by licensing their content to healthcare providers for patient education. We developed a systematic approach to packaging their episodes into themed modules, making it easier for organizations to integrate the content into their existing programs. This strategy not only generated significant licensing revenue but also helped establish the show as an authority in their field.

When developing your licensing strategy, consider these essential elements:

- Rights Management: Clearly define usage rights and restrictions
- Quality Control: Maintain oversight of how your content is used
- Revenue Models: Structure deals that provide fair compensation
- Distribution Tracking: Monitor where and how your content is used
- Brand Alignment: Ensure partners align with your show's values

Content syndication offers another powerful avenue for expanding your podcast's reach and revenue potential. Through strategic partnerships with relevant platforms and networks, you can expose your content to new audiences while maintaining control over your intellectual property.

I remember working with a financial education podcast that initially struggled with syndication strategy. We developed a tiered approach where certain episodes were widely syndicated while premium content remained exclusive to their primary platform. This balanced approach helped grow their audience while preserving the value of their core content.

Here are key considerations for successful content syndication:

- Platform Selection: Choose distribution partners that align with your target audience
- Content Strategy: Determine which content to syndicate versus keep exclusive
- Technical Requirements: Ensure your content meets platform specifications
- Monetization Terms: Understand revenue sharing and payment structures
- Analytics Integration: Track performance across multiple platforms

Remember that licensing and syndication deals require careful attention to legal details. Through my experience guiding podcasters through these agreements, I've learned the importance of clear contracts that protect both your interests and your content's integrity. Consider working with legal professionals who understand digital media rights when negotiating significant deals.

The most successful licensing and syndication strategies I've seen maintain a balance between accessibility and exclusivity. Your core podcast remains the primary platform for your content, while licensing and syndication serve as amplifiers that extend your reach and revenue potential.

One often overlooked aspect of content licensing is the opportunity for content adaptation. A cooking podcast I advised found success by licensing their content for use in culinary education programs, where their audio content was transformed into structured learning materials. This creative approach to licensing opened up entirely new revenue streams while reaching audiences in unexpected ways.

As you explore licensing and syndication opportunities, focus on partnerships that add value for your existing audience while attracting new listeners. The most sustainable deals are those that align with your show's mission and enhance rather than dilute your brand. Through strategic licensing and syndication, you can create multiple revenue streams from your existing content while building a stronger, more resilient podcast business.As we conclude our exploration of podcast monetization, it's worth reflecting on how far the medium has come since its early days. When podcasting first emerged in the early 2004 era, monetization was barely a consideration - creators were simply excited by the possibility of sharing their voices with the world through this new medium. The landscape has evolved dramatically since then, offering diverse opportunities for turning passion into profit while maintaining authenticity and audience trust.

Through my years of consulting, I've witnessed the transformation of podcast monetization from simple advertising models to sophisticated multi-stream revenue systems. The key lesson that emerges consistently is that sustainable podcast businesses rarely rely on a single income source. The most successful shows combine multiple revenue streams - from advertising and premium content to merchandise and consulting - creating a robust business model that can weather market changes and audience evolution.

My experience with the financial podcast client who transformed their modest 2,000-listener show into a thriving business through diversified revenue streams exemplifies the potential that exists beyond traditional advertising models. Their success didn't come from chasing larger audience numbers but from understanding and leveraging the unique value they offered their listeners. This approach - focusing on value creation rather than pure numbers - has become increasingly important in today's crowded podcast landscape.

As we look to the future of podcast monetization, the opportunities continue to expand. New technologies and platforms are creating innovative ways to generate revenue, while the growing acceptance of direct listener support models offers exciting possibilities for sustainable content creation. However, the fundamental principles remain constant: maintain authenticity, prioritize audience value, and build diverse revenue streams that align with your show's mission and goals.

Remember that successful monetization isn't just about implementing various revenue streams - it's about creating a sustainable ecosystem where each element supports and enhances the others. Whether through sponsorships, premium content, merchandise, consulting, or licensing, every monetization strategy should ultimately serve both your business goals and your audience's needs.

As you apply the strategies and insights from this chapter, focus on developing a monetization approach that reflects your unique voice and values while meeting your audience's expectations. Start small, test different approaches, and be willing to adapt based on results and feedback. Most importantly, never lose sight of the core reason you started podcasting - to share your voice and create value for your listeners.

The journey from passion project to profitable podcast may seem daunting, but with strategic planning, authentic audience engagement, and diversified revenue streams, you can build a sustainable podcast business that serves both your creative vision and financial goals. Remember, the most successful podcast monetization strategies are those that grow naturally from the value you create for your audience while staying true to your show's core mission and message.

7. Sustainable Success: Systems, Workflows, and Future-Proofing Your Show

The difference between podcasts that fizzle out after a few months and those that thrive for years often comes down to one critical factor: sustainable systems and workflows. While passion and creativity drive content creation, it's the behind-the-scenes infrastructure that enables consistent, high-quality production over the long haul. The heart of sustainable podcasting lies in developing systems that can weather the storms of technical challenges, creative blocks, and the ever-evolving media landscape. Having advised countless podcasters over my twenty-year consulting career, I've witnessed firsthand how the lack of robust workflows and systems can derail even the most promising shows. The transformation of podcasting from its early days of manual RSS feeds and basic audio hosting to today's sophisticated ecosystem of automation tools and content management platforms has created both opportunities and challenges for content creators.

During my second year as a marketing consultant, I encountered a client who was producing a successful weekly podcast but was constantly on the verge of burnout. Despite having great content and a growing audience, she was spending countless hours on repetitive tasks and struggling to maintain consistency. We sat down and mapped out her entire production process, identifying numerous inefficiencies and bottlenecks. Together, we developed a streamlined workflow system, created templates for common tasks, and implemented automation tools for social media and show notes. The transformation was remarkable - what once took her 15 hours per episode was reduced to just 6 hours, while actually improving the show's quality and consistency. Within three months, she was able to increase her episode frequency without adding stress to her schedule. This experience taught me the vital importance of systems and workflows in podcast sustainability. It's not just about working harder - it's about working smarter through well-designed processes and efficient systems.

In this chapter, we'll explore the critical components of building a sustainable podcast operation. From establishing efficient production workflows to implementing robust backup systems, you'll learn how to create a foundation that supports your show's growth while maintaining your sanity. We'll examine how successful podcasters leverage automation tools, content management systems, and scalable processes to ensure their shows can evolve with changing technology and audience expectations. Most importantly, you'll discover how to future-proof your podcast against the inevitable challenges and changes that come with long-term content creation.

Creating Efficient Production Workflows and Templates

Creating efficient workflows and templates is essential for maintaining a consistent, high-quality podcast without burning out. Early in my consulting career, I worked with a podcaster who spent nearly 20 hours producing each weekly episode. After analyzing her process, we discovered she was reinventing the wheel each time - writing show notes from scratch, creating social media posts on the fly, and repeatedly adjusting audio settings. By implementing a template-based system, we cut her production time by 60% while improving overall quality.

The foundation of an efficient podcast workflow starts with standardized templates. These should include:

- Episode planning documents with sections for topic research, guest information, and key talking points
- Show notes templates with consistent formatting and standard sections
- Social media post templates for different platforms
- Audio processing chains saved as DAW presets
- Email templates for guest outreach and follow-up

One of the most impactful changes you can make is establishing a production calendar that breaks down each episode into distinct phases. When I help clients develop their workflow, we typically divide the process into pre-production, recording, post-production, and promotion phases. Each phase should have its own checklist and standard operating procedures.

Pre-production efficiency comes from having clear templates and processes for research, outline creation, and guest coordination. I recommend creating a master episode planning document that includes sections for topic research, key talking points, technical requirements, and promotional strategy. This becomes your roadmap for each episode, ensuring nothing falls through the cracks.

The recording phase benefits enormously from having standardized technical settings and procedures. Create a recording checklist that covers everything from microphone placement to backup recording setup. Save your commonly used audio processing settings as presets in your Digital Audio Workstation (DAW). This ensures consistent sound quality across episodes while eliminating the need to recreate settings each time.

Post-production is where many podcasters get bogged down, but templates can dramatically streamline this process. Develop a standard episode structure with preset timing for intros, segues, and outros. Create template projects in your DAW with tracks already named and routed, effects chains in place, and standard mixing settings ready to go. This approach not only saves time but helps maintain consistent quality across episodes.

Promotion and distribution workflows should also be templatized. Create a promotional checklist that includes all platforms where you share your content, along with specific formatting requirements for each. Use social media scheduling tools to batch-create and schedule promotional posts. Maintain a template for show notes that includes standard sections like episode summaries, key quotes, and resource links.

Automation plays a crucial role in modern podcast workflows. Tools like Zapier or IFTTT can automate many repetitive tasks:

- Automatically posting to social media when episodes go live
- Creating draft blog posts from show notes
- Sending automated guest follow-up emails
- Generating transcripts using AI services

The key to successful workflow implementation is documentation. Create detailed standard operating procedures (SOPs) for each aspect of your production process. These SOPs should be clear enough that someone else could step in and maintain your show's quality standards if needed. This documentation becomes invaluable as your show grows and you potentially bring on team members.

Remember that workflows should evolve with your show. Regularly assess your processes to identify bottlenecks and opportunities for improvement. What works for a monthly show might need adjustment for weekly production, and solo shows have different requirements than interview formats. The goal is to create systems that are both efficient and flexible enough to grow with your podcast.

Perhaps most importantly, build quality control checkpoints into your workflow. These should include technical checks for audio quality, content reviews for accuracy and engagement, and final promotional material verification. Having these checkpoints systematized prevents errors while maintaining consistent quality across episodes.

Content Management Systems and Organization

Effective content management is the backbone of a sustainable podcast operation. Early in my consulting career, I worked with a podcast network that was struggling to manage content across multiple shows. Their scattered approach to file storage and episode organization led to lost recordings, version control issues, and countless hours spent searching for assets. This experience taught me the vital importance of implementing robust content management systems from day one.

A well-organized content management system (CMS) serves as your podcast's central nervous system, coordinating everything from raw audio files to finished episodes and promotional materials. When I help clients set up their CMS, we focus on creating a structured hierarchy that makes intuitive sense for their workflow. The goal is to establish a system that's both comprehensive and easy to navigate.

Here's what an effective podcast CMS should include:

- A clear folder structure for organizing episodes by season and number
- Dedicated spaces for raw audio, edited files, and final masters
- Asset libraries for music, sound effects, and promotional graphics
- Archived show notes and transcripts
- Guest information and release forms
- Technical documentation and equipment settings

The key to successful content organization lies in establishing consistent naming conventions. I recommend creating a standardized format that includes the episode number, date, and key identifiers. For example: 'EP042 *20240215* GuestName_Final.' This approach eliminates confusion and makes files instantly identifiable.

Cloud storage has revolutionized podcast content management, enabling seamless collaboration and providing crucial backup protection. When setting up cloud-based systems for clients, I emphasize the importance of regular synchronization and maintaining local backups of critical files. This redundancy has saved more than one show from disaster - I once had a client whose local drive failed the day before publication, but their cloud backup allowed them to recover and publish on schedule.

Version control is another critical aspect of content management. Maintain clear designations for different versions of your audio files, from rough cuts to final masters. I suggest using a simple system like 'V1,' 'V2,' 'FINAL' to track revisions. This prevents the common nightmare of accidentally publishing an unfinished version or losing critical edits.

Your CMS should also include a robust system for managing show notes, transcripts, and promotional materials. Create templates for these assets and store them alongside their corresponding episode files. This integrated approach ensures all episode-related content is easily accessible and properly organized.

Documentation plays a crucial role in content management. Maintain detailed records of your technical settings, processing chains, and production procedures. This documentation becomes invaluable when troubleshooting issues or onboarding new team members. I've seen countless podcasters struggle to recreate their sound after a technical failure simply because they hadn't documented their settings.

One often overlooked aspect of content management is asset organization. Create a centralized library for commonly used elements like intro music, transition effects, and branded graphics. This prevents the time-wasting practice of hunting through old episodes to find specific assets or, worse, having to recreate them from scratch.

Implementing a task management system alongside your CMS can significantly streamline your workflow. Whether you use dedicated project management software or a simple spreadsheet, having a clear system for tracking episode progress, deadlines, and responsibilities keeps your production on track. This becomes especially important as your show grows and you potentially bring on additional team members.

Remember that your content management system should grow and evolve with your show. Regularly review and refine your organization methods to ensure they continue serving your needs effectively. The time invested in maintaining a well-organized CMS pays dividends in reduced stress, improved efficiency, and consistent output quality.

Automation Tools and Time-Saving Techniques

In today's fast-paced podcasting landscape, automation tools have become essential for maintaining consistency and quality while reducing the time spent on repetitive tasks. When I first started consulting for podcasters, most production tasks were manual - from audio processing to social media posting. Now, the landscape has transformed dramatically with tools that can handle everything from scheduling to transcription automatically.

The key to effective podcast automation lies in identifying repetitive tasks that can be systematized without sacrificing quality. I learned this lesson working with a client who was spending hours manually posting show notes, creating social media content, and generating transcripts for each episode. By implementing a suite of automation tools, we reduced their post-production time by 70% while actually improving their content distribution consistency.

Here are the essential automation tools that every podcaster should consider:

- Scheduling and calendar tools for episode planning and guest coordination
- Social media automation platforms for content distribution
- Automated transcription services for accessibility and repurposing

- Email automation for guest communication and listener engagement
- RSS feed management tools for multi-platform distribution

The real power of automation comes from creating interconnected systems that work together seamlessly. For instance, when implementing automation for clients, I often set up workflows where publishing an episode automatically triggers social media posts, updates the show notes page, sends email notifications to subscribers, and generates transcripts. This integrated approach ensures consistent promotion across all channels without manual intervention.

Time-saving techniques extend beyond just automation tools. One of the most effective strategies I've implemented with clients is batch processing - recording multiple episodes in a single session while creative energy is high, then handling all the editing and post-production tasks together. This approach not only saves time but often results in more consistent quality across episodes.

Another crucial time-saving technique is the implementation of pre-production checklists and templates. Having standardized processes for research, outline creation, and guest preparation eliminates the need to reinvent the wheel for each episode. I've seen podcasters cut their preparation time in half simply by developing and following structured pre-production routines.

Audio processing automation has also evolved significantly. Modern Digital Audio Workstations (DAWs) offer powerful batch processing capabilities that can apply consistent audio enhancement across multiple episodes. Setting up automated processing chains for noise reduction, leveling, and compression not only saves time but ensures consistent sound quality across your entire show.

When implementing automation tools, it's crucial to maintain a balance between efficiency and personal touch. While automation can handle many routine tasks, certain elements of podcasting - like building genuine connections with guests and engaging with your community - should remain personal and authentic. I always advise clients to use automation to free up time for these high-value, relationship-building activities.

The future of podcast automation looks even more promising with the emergence of AI-powered tools. From content planning assistance to automated show notes generation, these technologies are making it easier than ever to maintain a consistent publishing schedule while focusing on creating compelling content. However, it's important to approach these tools as enhancers rather than replacements for human creativity and judgment.

Remember that automation should serve your podcast's goals, not dictate them. Start by automating the most time-consuming and repetitive tasks first, then gradually expand your automation toolkit as your show grows. Regular evaluation of your automated processes ensures they continue to serve your needs effectively while maintaining the quality standards your audience expects.

One often overlooked aspect of automation is the importance of proper setup and maintenance. Invest time in learning how to use your chosen tools effectively and regularly update your automated workflows to accommodate changes in your production process. This upfront investment pays dividends in long-term time savings and consistency.

Backup and Recovery Systems Implementation

In my twenty years of consulting, I've witnessed countless podcasters learn the hard way about the critical importance of backup systems - often after suffering devastating content losses. One particularly memorable case involved a client who lost three months of carefully crafted episodes due to a single hard drive failure. This experience fundamentally shaped how I approach backup strategy with every podcaster I work with.

A robust backup and recovery system is your podcast's insurance policy against technical disasters, human error, and the unexpected challenges that inevitably arise in content creation. The key is implementing multiple layers of protection that work together seamlessly to ensure your content is always safe and recoverable.

Here are the essential components of a comprehensive podcast backup system:

- Automated local backups of all raw recordings
- Cloud storage synchronization for project files
- Redundant recording during live sessions
- Archive system for completed episodes
- Documentation backup for show notes and scripts
- Regular system verification and testing

The 3-2-1 backup rule forms the foundation of any solid backup strategy. This means maintaining three copies of your content, stored on two different types of media, with one copy kept off-site. In practice, this might mean having your primary files on your computer, a local external drive backup, and cloud storage synchronization.

When implementing backup systems for clients, I emphasize the importance of automation. Manual backups are prone to human error and often get neglected during busy production periods. Setting up automated backup software that runs in the background ensures your content is protected without requiring constant attention.

Recording redundancy is another crucial aspect of podcast backup strategy. During recording sessions, always maintain at least two separate recording sources. This might mean using your primary recording software while simultaneously recording to a portable device, or utilizing backup recording features in your remote recording platform. This redundancy has saved countless episodes from technical glitches that would have otherwise required complete re-recording.

Cloud storage plays a vital role in modern podcast backup systems, but it's important to understand its limitations. While services like Dropbox, Google Drive, or dedicated podcast hosting platforms provide excellent backup options, they shouldn't be your only line of defense. I recommend maintaining local backups of all critical files alongside cloud storage solutions.

Organization is key to effective backup management. Implement a clear folder structure and naming convention for your backup files that makes it easy to locate specific content when needed. Include version numbers and dates in your file names, and maintain a log of backup activities and verifications.

Regular testing of your backup systems is essential but often overlooked. Schedule monthly checks to verify that your backups are working correctly and that you can actually restore files when needed. I've seen too many podcasters discover their backup systems weren't functioning properly only when they needed them most.

Your backup strategy should also include your show's supporting materials. This means maintaining copies of:

- Show notes and scripts
- Guest release forms and contracts
- Technical documentation and settings
- Promotional materials and artwork
- Email correspondence and planning documents

Recovery procedures are just as important as backup systems. Document step-by-step recovery processes for different scenarios, from single file restoration to complete system recovery. This documentation should be stored both digitally and in hard copy, accessible even if your main systems are down.

Consider implementing a version control system for your episode files. This allows you to track changes and revert to previous versions if needed. While this might seem like overkill for a podcast, it can be invaluable when dealing with complex episodes or collaborative projects.

Remember that backup needs evolve as your show grows. Regularly review and update your backup strategy to ensure it continues to meet your changing requirements. What works for a monthly show might need enhancement for weekly production, and solo shows have different backup needs than interview formats.

The investment in robust backup systems might seem excessive until you need them. However, the time and effort saved when recovering from a technical disaster far outweigh the initial setup costs. As I often tell my clients, it's not a question of if you'll need your backups, but when.

Scalable Operations and Team Management

As your podcast grows, the need for efficient team management and scalable operations becomes increasingly important. In my consulting practice, I've witnessed many successful solo podcasters struggle with the transition to managing a team and scaling their operations. One memorable client went from producing a weekly show alone to managing a network of three shows with a team of five in just eight months. The growth was exciting but nearly derailed their entire operation due to unclear roles and inconsistent processes.

The key to successful podcast scaling lies in building systems that can grow with your show while maintaining quality and consistency. When I help clients prepare for growth, we focus on creating clear operational frameworks that can accommodate additional team members and increased production demands without sacrificing the show's core value proposition.

Here are the fundamental elements of scalable podcast operations:

- Clearly defined roles and responsibilities
- Documented standard operating procedures
- Communication protocols and project management systems
- Quality control checkpoints
- Training and onboarding procedures
- Performance metrics and feedback systems

The transition from solo operation to team management requires a shift in mindset. As a solo podcaster, you might keep most processes in your head, but scaling requires explicit documentation and systematization. I learned this lesson early in my consulting career when helping a client expand their production team. We spent weeks documenting every aspect of their production process, from initial research to final publication, creating detailed guides that new team members could follow.

Team management in podcasting presents unique challenges due to the creative nature of the medium. When building teams for clients, I emphasize the importance of balancing creative freedom with consistent production standards. This means establishing clear guidelines while leaving room for individual contribution and innovation.

One effective approach to team scaling is the pod system, where small groups handle specific aspects of production. For instance, you might have one pod focused on content research and planning, another on technical production, and a third on promotion and community engagement. This structure allows for specialization while maintaining manageable team sizes.

Communication becomes increasingly critical as your team grows. Implement regular check-ins and status updates, but be careful not to over-burden the creative process with excessive meetings. I recommend using project management tools that provide visibility into project status without requiring constant direct communication. This allows team members to stay informed while focusing on their core responsibilities.

Quality control becomes more complex with a larger team, but it's essential for maintaining consistent output. Establish clear review processes and approval workflows that ensure all content meets your standards without creating bottlenecks. Consider implementing a tiered review system where experienced team members can approve certain elements while you maintain final oversight of critical components.

Training and onboarding new team members requires significant upfront investment but pays dividends in long-term operational efficiency. Create comprehensive onboarding documents that cover both technical skills and your show's creative vision. Include practical exercises and shadowing opportunities to help new team members understand your production standards and workflow.

As your operation scales, pay particular attention to:

- Resource allocation and scheduling
- Team member skill development
- Cross-training opportunities
- Workflow optimization
- Technology infrastructure scaling
- Budget management and cost control

Remember that scaling isn't just about adding more people - it's about building systems that enable growth while maintaining quality. One client's attempt to scale quickly by simply hiring more people without proper systems in place led to confusion, inconsistent output, and ultimately, the need to rebuild their entire operation from the ground up.

Regularly assess your operational capacity and identify potential bottlenecks before they become problems. This might mean investing in additional equipment, upgrading software systems, or bringing on specialized team members to handle specific aspects of production. The goal is to stay ahead of growth rather than constantly playing catch-up.

Finally, maintain clear communication channels for feedback and improvement suggestions from your team. Some of the most valuable operational improvements I've seen came from team members who were directly involved in day-to-day production. Create an environment where everyone feels empowered to contribute ideas for improving efficiency and quality.

Remember that scaling operations is a gradual process. Start with the most critical areas that need support and expand systematically. This measured approach allows you to maintain control over quality while building a sustainable operation that can continue growing with your podcast's success.

Future-Proofing: Adapting to Industry Changes

The podcasting landscape has evolved dramatically since its inception when RSS feeds first enabled audio content distribution. As a marketing consultant who witnessed this evolution firsthand, I've seen the industry transform from simple MP3 files shared through basic RSS feeds to today's sophisticated ecosystem of streaming platforms, analytics, and monetization tools. This constant evolution underscores a crucial truth: the only constant in podcasting is change.

Early in my consulting career, I worked with a client who insisted on using only direct MP3 downloads through their website, refusing to adapt to emerging podcast platforms. Within a year, their listenership had plummeted as audiences shifted to consuming content through dedicated podcast apps. This experience taught me a valuable lesson about the importance of staying adaptable in an evolving media landscape.

Future-proofing your podcast requires a balanced approach between embracing new technologies and maintaining core quality standards. Here are the key areas to focus on for long-term sustainability:

- Platform diversification and distribution strategy
- Technical infrastructure flexibility
- Content format adaptability
- Audience engagement evolution
- Monetization model diversity
- Emerging technology adoption

The key to successful future-proofing lies in building flexible systems that can adapt to change without requiring complete overhauls. When I help clients develop their long-term strategy, we focus on creating modular approaches to production and distribution that can evolve with the industry. This might mean investing in equipment that supports multiple formats, developing content that can be easily repurposed across platforms, or building audience engagement systems that can scale with new technologies.

One of the most effective future-proofing strategies is maintaining format flexibility. While audio remains the core of podcasting, successful shows increasingly need to think about how their content can adapt to emerging formats. This doesn't mean chasing every new trend, but rather ensuring your production workflow can accommodate different content delivery methods as they become relevant to your audience.

Technical infrastructure plays a crucial role in future-proofing. I recommend clients maintain systems that can easily integrate with new tools and platforms. This might mean choosing hosting providers with robust APIs, using content management systems that support multiple export formats, or implementing backup systems that preserve content in various file formats for future use.

Audience engagement strategies must also evolve with changing consumption patterns. The rise of social audio platforms and interactive content has shown how quickly audience expectations can shift. Building direct relationships with your audience through email lists, community platforms, and other owned channels provides stability amid platform changes.

Monetization diversity is another critical aspect of future-proofing. Relying too heavily on any single revenue stream can leave your podcast vulnerable to industry shifts. I've seen shows struggle when platform algorithms change or advertising markets fluctuate.

Developing multiple revenue streams - from direct support to premium content to merchandise - creates resilience against market changes.

Perhaps most importantly, stay informed about industry trends without becoming reactive to every new development. Subscribe to industry newsletters, participate in podcasting communities, and maintain relationships with other creators. This network can provide early insights into meaningful changes while helping filter out temporary trends.

Remember that future-proofing isn't about predicting the future - it's about building systems flexible enough to adapt to whatever changes come. When I first started consulting, podcasting was primarily about audio files and RSS feeds. Now it encompasses video podcasting, live streaming, social audio, and formats we couldn't have imagined. The shows that have thrived through these changes are those that maintained core quality while strategically embracing new opportunities.

Regular audits of your technical stack, content strategy, and audience engagement methods help identify areas that might need updating. Schedule quarterly reviews of your systems and processes, asking questions like: Are our current tools meeting our needs? How are audience consumption patterns changing? What new technologies or platforms should we be exploring?

The future of podcasting will likely bring more changes - from advances in AI and automation to new content formats and distribution methods. Building adaptability into your podcast's foundation ensures you can navigate these changes while maintaining the core value you provide to your audience. The goal isn't to chase every trend but to position your show to take advantage of meaningful opportunities as they arise.As we conclude this chapter on sustainable systems and future-proofing your podcast, I'm reminded of how far the medium has come since those early days of RSS feeds and basic MP3 downloads. When podcasting first emerged, just a little over two decades ago, few could have predicted its evolution into today's sophisticated ecosystem of streaming platforms, automated tools, and diverse monetization opportunities. Yet through all these changes, one truth has remained constant: successful podcasts are built on solid foundations of sustainable systems and adaptable workflows.

The journey from casual creator to professional podcaster requires more than just passionate content creation - it demands thoughtful implementation of efficient workflows, robust backup systems, and scalable operations. Throughout this chapter, we've explored how to build these crucial systems while maintaining the flexibility to evolve with industry changes. From creating efficient production workflows and implementing comprehensive content management systems to establishing redundant backup protocols and future-proof distribution strategies, each element plays a vital role in long-term podcast sustainability.

Perhaps most importantly, we've learned that sustainable podcasting isn't about working harder - it's about working smarter. By implementing the systems and workflows outlined in this chapter, you can focus more energy on creating compelling content while ensuring your show maintains consistent quality and reliability. The automation tools, time-saving techniques, and team management strategies we've discussed provide a framework for growth without sacrificing the unique voice and perspective that makes your podcast special.

As I reflect on my decades of experience in digital marketing and podcasting, I'm continually amazed by the industry's evolution and the new opportunities it presents for content creators. Yet the fundamental principles of sustainable podcast production remain unchanged: clear systems, efficient workflows, reliable backups, and adaptable strategies. These elements form the foundation upon which successful podcasts are built and maintained.

Remember that building sustainable systems is an ongoing process, not a one-time task. Regularly review and refine your workflows, stay informed about industry developments, and maintain flexibility in your approach. The podcasting landscape will continue to evolve, but with robust systems in place, your show will be well-positioned to adapt and thrive in whatever the future holds.

As you move forward with your podcasting journey, let the principles and strategies outlined in this chapter guide you in creating not just great content, but a sustainable and scalable podcast operation that can weather any challenges while continuing to serve and grow your audience. The future of podcasting is bright, and with the right systems in place, your show can be part of that future for years to come.

Conclusion

As we reach the end of our podcasting journey together, it's worth reflecting on how far this medium has come since its humble beginnings. When Dave Winer and Adam Curry created the first RSS feed for audio content in 2004, they couldn't have imagined that their innovation would evolve into a global phenomenon reaching billions of listeners. From those early days of experimental technology to today's sophisticated podcast landscape, one truth has remained constant: the power of authentic voices to connect, engage, and inspire.

Throughout this book, we've explored every aspect of podcast creation and growth - from selecting your first microphone to building multiple revenue streams. We've delved into the technical foundations that make great audio possible, examined content strategies that keep listeners coming back, and uncovered marketing approaches that help your show find its audience. The journey from concept to successful podcast isn't always straightforward, but the path is now clearer than ever before.

What excites me most about podcasting's future is its continued democratization of media. Whether you're an entrepreneur sharing business insights, a hobbyist discussing vintage video games, or a storyteller crafting audio narratives, there's space for your voice in the podcast universe. The barriers to entry have never been lower, while the potential for impact and growth has never been higher.

Your success in podcasting won't be determined by having the most expensive equipment or the largest initial audience. Instead, it will come from your commitment to authenticity, your willingness to learn and adapt, and your dedication to serving your listeners with valuable content. Remember that every successful podcaster started exactly where you are now - with an idea, a desire to connect, and the courage to press record.

The systems, strategies, and insights shared in this book provide a foundation, but your unique voice and perspective will build something truly special upon that foundation. As you begin or continue your podcasting journey, stay curious, remain persistent, and never stop learning. The podcast landscape will continue to evolve, but the fundamental principles of creating value for your audience will always remain relevant.

In my twenty years of consulting, I've watched countless podcasts grow from modest beginnings into influential platforms that transform both creators and listeners. Your podcast has the same potential. Whether your goals involve building a community, sharing expertise, or creating a sustainable business, the tools and knowledge you need are now in your hands.

As you move forward, remember that every successful podcast is built one episode at a time. Focus on consistent improvement rather than immediate perfection. Engage with your audience, learn from feedback, and stay true to your unique voice. The podcast world is waiting for what only you can create - so get out there and say it!

Bibliography

Curry, A. & Winer, D. (2004). RSS 2.0 Specification. Retrieved from https://cyber.harvard.edu/rss/rss.html

Edison Research. (2023). The Infinite Dial 2023. Retrieved from https://www.edisonresearch.com/the-infinite-dial-2023/

Friends, B. (2005). Podcasting and Portable Media. New Riders Press.

Hammersley, B. (2004, February 12). Audible Revolution. The Guardian. Retrieved from https://www.theguardian.com/media/2004/feb/12/broadcasting.digitalmedia

International Podcast Association. (2023). Podcast Industry Standards and Best Practices Guide. Retrieved from https://www.internationalpodcast.org/standards

Podcast Index. (2023). Podcast Namespace Specification. Retrieved from https://github.com/Podcastindex-org/podcast-namespace

Voice Audio Network. (2023). State of Podcast Advertising Report. Retrieved from https://www.voiceaudionetwork.com/reports

www.ingramcontent.com/pod-product-compliance
Lightning Source LLC
LaVergne TN
LVHW081801050326
832903LV00027B/2041